O9-CFT-676

THE COMPLETE GUIDE TO
RUBBER STAMPING

WATSON-GUPTILL CRAFTS

THE COMPLETE GUIDE TO
RUBBER STAMPING

DESIGN AND DECORATE GIFTS AND KEEPSAKES
SIMPLY AND BEAUTIFULLY WITH RUBBER STAMPS

GRACE TAORMINA

WATSON-GUPTILL PUBLICATIONS/NEW YORK

Senior Editor: Candace Raney
Edited by Joy Aquilino
Designed by Areta Buk
Graphic production by Ellen Greene

Copyright © 1996 by Rubber Stampede

First published in 1996 by Watson-Guptill Publications,
a division of BPI Communications, Inc.,
1515 Broadway, New York, N.Y. 10036

Library of Congress Cataloging-in-Publication Data

Taormina, Grace.
    The complete guide to rubber stamping : design and decorate gifts
and keepsakes simply and beautifully with rubber stamps / Grace
Taormina.
        p.   cm.
    Includes index.
    ISBN 0-8230-4613-3 (paper)
    1. Rubber stamp printing.   I. Title.
TT867.T36   1996
761—dc20   96-3256
                                                                CIP

All rights reserved. No part of this publication may be reproduced or
used in any form or by any means—graphic, electronic, or mechanical,
including photocopying, recording, taping, or information storage and
retrieval systems—without written permission of the publisher.

Manufactured in Singapore

First printing, 1996

4 5 6 7 8 9 / 04 03 02 01 00 99 98 97

ACKNOWLEDGMENTS

My deepest gratitude to the following people, whose contributions made this book possible:

Sam and Tsoi Katzen, for their vision and dedication to providing an innovative and creative atmosphere in which to try out new ideas;

Scott Wooden and Kathleen O'Connell, for their ideas, advice, faith, and words of encouragement;

Merja Lehtinen, for her creative and technical advice;

Suze Weinberg and Dee Gruenig, for sharing their contagious enthusiasm and technical expertise in the art of rubber stamping;

Clara Arriaga, Lorenzo Becerra, Lynn Damelio, Guadalupe Martinez, Susanna Espinoza, Dung Nguyuen, Aida Segura, Aida Simbe, Samantha Starr, and Karla Tempest, for their talent, skill, and dedication in producing the samples for the projects;

Estela Celestino, Melody Cretin, Joann Miller, Erin Shetterly, and Sydney Thatcher, for assisting with all the numerous details;

Joy Aquilino, for her magic with words;

my family and friends, for their moral support;

and my husband Sal and children Joey and Rachel, for their love, understanding, and patience during this chapter of creative chaos in our lives.

CONTRIBUTING DESIGNERS
Clara Arriaga
Lynn Damelio
Dee Gruenig
Elena Moore
Michelle Powell
Samantha Starr
Debora Tanaka
Grace Taormina
Linda Watson
Suze Weinberg

PHOTOGRAPHERS
David Belda
Sal Taormina

ILLUSTRATOR
Donna Yuen

CONTENTS

Introduction   8

MATERIALS AND SUPPLIES   10

Stamp Basics   12
Inks and Stamp Pads   16
Stamping Surfaces   19
Tools and Supplies   24

STAMPING TECHNIQUES   30

Inking a Stamp   32
Positioning a Stamp Accurately   34
Embossing   36
Working with Paper   37
Design Strategies   38
Color Fundamentals   42
Working with Color   46
Masking   48
Creating Depth and Dimension   51
Creating Motion   53
Backgrounds   56
Borders and Edges   58

PAPER PROJECTS   60

African Wildlife Gift Wrap   62
Stained Glass Grape Card   64
Hydrangea Gift Wrap   66
Mixed-Pattern Notecard   68
Red Rose Stationery Set   70
Stamped Watercolor Art Cards   74
Paper Jewelry   76

HOME DECOR 78

Embossed Animal Skin Print Mats 80
Autumn Leaves Frame 82
Butterfly Box 84
Melamine Vegetable Plates 86
Decorative Terracotta Tiles 88

GIFT IDEAS 90

Japanese Paper Gift Boxes 92
Fern Stationery and Gift Box 94
Fern Frame and Gift Wrap 96
Japanese Journal 98
Border-Pattern T-Shirt 100
Recipe Box Gift Set 102
Celestial Treasure Box and Gift Tag 105

STAMPING FOR STITCHERS 108

Linen and Lace Victorian Posy Pillow 110
Quilted Garden Wall Hanging 112
Miniature Pieced Quilt 114
Primitive Art Wall Hanging 116
Counting Sheep Pillow 118
Clay Button Wall Hanging 121

HOLIDAYS AND SPECIAL OCCASIONS 124

Birthday Party Accessories 126
Romantic Valentine's Day Collage 128
Calla Lily Notecard 130
Halloween Pop-Up Card 132
Christmas Ornament Card 134
Gingerbread Apron 136
Quilted Holiday Stockings 138
Dimensional Partridge Picture 140
Découpage Angel Tray 142
New Year's Eve Party Invitation 144

Patterns and Diagrams 146
Source Directory 156
Index 157

INTRODUCTION

Welcome to the world of rubber stamping! Stamping is an amazingly simple and versatile way to express your creativity. This book explores rubber stamping's boundless potential in depth. By practicing the techniques and completing just a few of the projects, you'll discover that rubber stamping can inspire you to formulate your own designs and produce original projects.

Rubber stamps have been used for many years as practical marking devices. We're all familiar with date stamps used to check out library books, "date received" stamps used to mark incoming office mail, and bookkeeping stamps used to mark invoices as paid or past due. With the development of sophisticated manufacturing technology, highly detailed images are now being produced as rubber stamps, opening up a new world of creative possibilities.

While conducting workshops and demonstrations, I'm always delighted to observe the extent to which simple rubber stamp techniques can captivate an audience: the immediate satisfaction that can be found in making "instant art," the "magic" of thermal embossing, the visual possibilities of masking—in short, combining rubber stamps with "ordinary" materials and techniques to create something extraordinary. This is just one of the reasons for the recent surge in rubber stamping's popularity.

It became apparent from the many inquiries I receive from people who have explored rubber stamping that there was a demand for a book that answers fundamental questions and can help resolve uncertainty. The purpose of *The Complete Guide to Rubber Stamping* is to provide novice stampers with an introduction to this wonderful craft, from how rubber stamps are made, maintained, and stored, to how each medium and tool can be used to obtain a specific result. In addition, stampers at all levels of experience will find valuable information on strategies for design and color, such as how to compose a layout or pattern, and how color can be used to affect perception and suggest depth within a composition. If you're an artist or a crafter with an established area of interest, you'll find that rubber stamps can be used with practically every art or craft medium, including fabric, wood, clay, or just plain paper.

The heart of this book is devoted to a wide range of projects, featuring various images, stamping styles and techniques, color schemes, and surfaces. A complete materials list and step-by-step instructions are provided for each project so that you can duplicate the finished objects exactly as they appear. Above all, I encourage you to use the projects as springboards for exploring your own ideas and developing your own style, adapting them to the stamp images and materials you have on hand.

While there is some debate about the artistic value of stamping, since it merely reproduces an image created by someone else, a stamped image can become art when it is used to make an original, inventive, and innovative piece of work. Each combination of stamp images, inks, colors, accessories, and surfaces reflects the stamper's individuality. Don't worry if your first prints aren't exactly what you expected. As with all things, a little practice is all you need. Sometimes you'll find that the unexpected is far superior to what you had originally planned.

Rubber stamping is also an excellent medium for recycling. For example, when embellished with stamped prints in bright colors, a plain paper bag can serve as a gift bag. When cut up and combined with stamped images, discarded papers and old gift wrap can be used to make an eclectic collage. A stain on a T-shirt or tablecloth can be camouflaged with a pattern stamped in fabric inks. A common terracotta flowerpot can be transformed into a gift by personalizing it with letter stamps.

Rubber stamps are truly creative tools. With so many thousands of images available, there are virtually no limits on what you can make. With rubber stamping, *you* are the designer and artist: Your choices—images, colors, and surface—express *your* creativity. Have fun, explore, and discover. Happy stamping!

FAIR USE: A NOTE ON COPYRIGHT LAW

It's important for all stampers to understand how the issues of copyright protection and infringement apply to the rubber stamp industry. The use of a rubber stamp that is purchased from a retail or wholesale source must be confined to personal, noncommercial, and nonprofit applications. This means that you cannot use rubber stamps to make business stationery, advertisements, or products such as greeting cards or postcards for resale unless you receive permission from the stamp manufacturer. To do so without permission would be copyright infringement.

A rubber stamp manufacturer produces stamps from original artwork created by both in-house and freelance illustrators. They either purchase a design outright or license it from an artist in return for a percentage of its sales. Some companies also manufacture and distribute rubber stamps featuring well-known copyrighted cartoon and celebrity images. As licensees, these companies pay a fee for the exclusive right to produce these images as well as a percentage of their sales to the licenser, and are usually required by the licenser to follow certain standards in order to maintain the integrity of the images.

Because rubber stamp companies make large investments in their artwork and licensed images, they will protect their property if it is infringed upon. Note that a few rubber stamp companies will grant permission to use their images for commercial use. If you use rubber stamps images to decorate items that you intend to sell, it is recommended that you contact each manufacturer directly to resolve any questions you might have regarding their commercial use.

MATERIALS AND SUPPLIES

One of stamping's most appealing qualities is that a beginner can get started with a very low investment in essential equipment. All that's required are rubber stamps, inks (stamp pads and/or markers), and a stamping surface. As you discover new creative possibilities by experimenting with different techniques, you'll want to add other supplies to your collection. Most of the items discussed in this chapter can be purchased at art supply, crafts, and stationery stores, as well as at retail stores that specialize in rubber stamp supplies and accessories. If you can't find a local retail source for your supplies, or if you can't find something that's used in one of the projects in this book, consult the source directory (pages 156–157) for more information.

STAMP BASICS

There are literally thousands of rubber stamp images available to express every interest and occasion. Most people start their collections with simple images such as stars, hearts, or balloons to decorate correspondence, name stamps to personalize their belongings, or word stamps to convey a sentiment. Others center their collections around a specific subject, such as teddy bears, flowers, or scenery. Most stamps can be classified as one of two types: basic outline and broad-surface.

- *Outline stamps* make imprints of an image's outline, which can then be colored in with markers or pencils. Outline stamps may include some details, such as simplified highlights or shading. Cartoon and character stamps are good examples of outline stamps.
- *Broad-surface stamps* use a solid mass of rubber to imprint an image, thus eliminating the need for any additional coloring. Designs can range from simple shapes to moderately detailed images. Many word stamps fall into this category.

ANATOMY OF A RUBBER STAMP

A rubber stamp is made by molding an image into rubber and mounting it on a wood, thick foam, plastic, or Plexiglas block or roller. Discussed on pages 13–14 are other types of stamps made from various materials, some of which are

Examples of the two primary types of stamps: an outline stamp (top) and a broad-surface stamp (bottom).

unmounted. It is also possible to carve small stamps from erasers, and large ones from wood, linoleum, a number of synthetic foams, sponges, and even potatoes. Because wood-handled rubber stamps are well made, durable, easy to use and to clean, and aesthetically pleasing objects in and of themselves, the projects in this book feature them exclusively. Here we will focus primarily on how rubber stamps are made and the characteristics of a good rubber stamp.

A wood-handled rubber stamp is traditionally made up of three components:

1. *The die* is the rubber design. The rubber is most commonly red, pink, or gray. The image should be deeply etched into the rubber so that it makes clean, clear prints.
2. *The cushion* is the padding between the die and the wood block. The cushion, which is usually made of foam, should be thick enough to elevate the die so that the wood block does not come in contact with the stamping surface. The cushion's other important function is to evenly disperse the pressure placed on the stamp to all parts of the die.
3. *The block* or *mount* is the wood handle to which the die and cushion are attached. High-quality stamps feature hardwood blocks, typically maple. Some blocks have finger grips that make them more comfortable to hold.

HOW RUBBER STAMPS ARE MADE

Die designs are created from original artwork, either hand-drawn or computer-generated illustrations. Some companies use copyright-free designs, both "as is" or with slight modifications so that they can claim the designs as their own. Designs produced by rubber stamp companies are copyrighted, so they cannot be used for commercial purposes. (For more information, see "Fair Use: A Note on Copyright Law," page 9.)

The final artwork is then photographed to create a negative. The negative film is transformed by a platemaking machine to create a master mold, which is then used to create several production molds. Skilled technicians then place the production molds and sheets of blank "raw" rubber into a machine called a *vulcanizer.* The vulcanizer has two metal plates that sandwich the molds and rubber together, exerting several tons of pressure and heating the rubber to high temperatures so that it melts and oozes into the molds. The rubber is then cooled and removed from the molds.

The sheets of vulcanized rubber are glued to a thin, flexible foam cushion. The individual images are then cut out and affixed to wood blocks that have been indexed (stamped) with the image in permanent ink. Some companies index their stamps by affixing a color label of the image to the block. Because the labels sometimes fall off after extended use, new technology has been developed to print color images directly on the block, thus increasing the longevity and attractiveness of the stamp.

Many stamp companies sell rubber dies, cushions, and blocks separately. Unmounted stamps are usually significantly less expensive because you supply the labor in assembling and indexing the stamps.

OTHER TYPES OF STAMPS

As you seek to expand your collection of images, you may want to experiment with other types of stamps.

- *Foam-handled stamps,* which are typically less expensive than wood-handled stamps, are a good way to obtain a collection of several images at a reasonable price. Most rubber stamp kits contain rubber dies mounted on thick foam instead of wood. Care must be taken when using these stamps to avoid leaving an impression of the edges of the foam handle on your project, which is called a *backprint*. Some stamp collectors safeguard against this by trimming the foam with a craft knife, or by removing the rubber dies from the foam and remounting them on wood.

- *Clear-mount stamps* feature polymer (a type of plastic) instead of rubber dies and are mounted on clear Plexiglas blocks. Because you can see through the Plexiglas *and* the die, this type of stamp allows you to make very precise placements without using a stamp positioning tool (see pages 34–35).
- *Roller stamps* consist of a single-strip die molded with several designs that is mounted on a plastic roller so that a continuous series of images is printed as it is rolled across the stamping surface.
- *Shared-mount stamps* feature mounts made of such materials as magnets and Velcro, so that one mount can be used for several images. These stamps are economical and great space savers.

STAMP CARE AND MAINTENANCE

Rubber stamps will last indefinitely if you take care of them. Keep them clean by thoroughly removing ink with stamp cleaner or water after every use. Other effective cleaners are baby wipes (without alcohol) and diluted window cleaner (without ammonia). Since there are many different inks and stamp cleaners on the market, you should always follow the manufacturer's instructions for the safest and most effective cleaning procedure.

To keep your stamps clean while you are working on a project, set up a paper towel moistened with stamp cleaner or water in a flat plastic tray, then place a couple of layers of dry paper towels next to the tray. When you finish using your stamp, stamp it on the moistened towel a few times, then blot it on a dry paper towel. Repeat until the rubber no longer shows traces of ink. If you've been less than meticulous about stamp care, you may find it helpful to use an old toothbrush to clean dried ink out of a stamp's crevices.

Never immerse your stamps in water or use any solvent-based cleaners on your stamps, as this may loosen the adhesive used to mount the stamps on the wood block. Keep your stamps away from sunlight or the rubber will dry out and become brittle, which will diminish the clarity and precision of your prints.

ORGANIZING AND STORING YOUR STAMPS

Whether you're a beginner or an experienced stamper, one of stamping's most challenging dilemmas is how to keep your stamps and accessories organized. As your collection grows and you begin to accumulate the vast array of stamps and stamping supplies now available, finding a way to store and keep track of them will become an issue. Described below are a few of the simpler and more inexpensive storage strategies developed over several years of stamping experience. Try them and see what works for you.

If you're just starting out, you'll probably need just one box to store your stamps, ink pads, and accessories. As your collection grows, it will become necessary to categorize your images and store each category in a separate box. Start by dividing them into major categories, such as animals, florals, scenery, insects, cartoon characters, body parts, vegetables, fruit, hearts, individual words, sentiments, alphabets, and so forth. As your collection expands, these categories can then be subcategorized; for example, "animals" can be sorted into dogs, cats, birds, and so on.

Among the easily obtainable boxes and containers that work well for storing stamps are shoe boxes, flat boxes with lids, letter trays from stationery stores, acrylic box frames from frame stores, and plastic food-storage containers, as well as any of the various commercial drawer-organizing systems currently on the market. Also, several rubber stamp suppliers now manufacture acrylic drawers and shelves specifically for storing stamps. Some stampers prefer to see their stamps at all times. Narrow wall shelves, acrylic shelves, and old printer trays are all great ways to store and display your stamps.

Regardless of which type of container you choose, you should label your boxes on the front so that when they are stacked you can immediately identify their contents. To keep stamps organized within each container, cut a blank piece of paper so that it fits inside the bottom of the box. Arrange your stamps in the container, make an outline of each wood block, then stamp each stamp in the appropriate box. To keep the paper clean, cover it with clear contact paper. With this method of organization, each stamp has its own place and can be readily found the next time you need it.

Store any masks you make along with their corresponding stamps so you can locate them quickly. (See "Masking," pages 48–50.) If you use a stamp positioning tool frequently, you can also store the tissue paper template used with the tool with its corresponding stamp. (See "Positioning a Stamp Accurately," pages 34–35.)

Acrylic boxes are an excellent way to store stamps. To keep stamps organized within each container, draw an outline of each wood block on a sheet of paper, then stamp each image in its corresponding outline.

INKS AND STAMP PADS

The traditional dye-based felt stamp pad is the type of ink that most people immediately envision when the words "rubber stamp" are mentioned. As a result of the increasing popularity of rubber stamping, many types of inks and an assortment of stamp pads in various shapes and sizes are now offered. The type of ink and stamp pad you choose will depend largely on your project's surface.

INKS

There are five primary types of inks used for stamping: dye-based, pigment, embossing, fabric, and permanent. These are the traditional stamping inks, but adventurous stampers often try other substances, including acrylic and craft paints, glue, and bleach, to stamp a variety of surfaces. The potential applications of some of these nontraditional "inks" are explored in some of the projects in this book.

DYE-BASED INKS

If you've done any stamping, chances are you've used a dye-based ink. Dye-based inks are water-based and are usually manufactured along with a felt stamp pad. Most come in plastic cases with hinged or removable tops, and can range in size

A multicolored selection of inks, stamp pads, and re-inkers, including dye-based and pigment inks; permanent and washable inks; translucent and opaque inks; and rainbow, small, and uninked stamp pads.

from 1-inch squares to very large rectangles. Dye-based ink pads are available in a variety of colors, including rainbow pads. Some companies sell washable dye-based inks made specifically for children.

Dye-based inks, which are translucent, dry quickly and can be stamped on most types of papers. Images will look crisper and colors brighter when stamped on white, glossy coated papers, and more opaque when stamped on uncoated paper stock. Because dye-based inks are water-based, they may bleed or blur on very absorbent papers. Stamps printed with these inks will fade with time, especially when exposed to light.

PIGMENT INKS
Pigment inks are thick, opaque, almost paste-like inks, and are usually paired with foam stamp pads. They are available in a multitude of sizes and colors, including metallics.

Pigment inks stamp well on all types of paper and resist fading, so they are suitable for use with archival materials. Because they have a thick consistency, pigment inks look rich and vibrant even on colored paper stock, and won't dry on coated papers unless they are embossed. Although their drying time is significantly longer than for dye-based inks, they can be used without embossing on uncoated papers.

EMBOSSING INKS
Embossing inks, which are glycerin-based, are usually clear or slightly tinted and can be applied to either felt or foam stamp pads. These inks are designed to dry slowly so that embossing powder will adhere to the stamped image. Colored and metallic embossing powders are usually used with embossing inks. Embossing ink can also be used as a resist. (See "Embossing," page 36; and "Backgrounds," pages 56–57.)

FABRIC INKS
Available in both water- and solvent-based formulations, fabric inks are made specifically for use on fabrics. Some brands must be set with heat in order to be made permanent on fabrics, though most can also be used on other surfaces such as wood and clay without heat. Thicker in consistency than dye-based inks, fabric inks are usually sold in bottles with an accompanying felt stamp pad. Some manufacturers package their fabric inks in bottles with rounded felt tops so that the ink can be dabbed directly onto the rubber stamp. Some stampers prefer to spread fabric ink on a piece of glass and use a rubber brayer to apply it evenly to the stamp, while others apply the ink with a wedge-shaped foam sponge or a small sponge brush. The method you choose depends on your personal preference as well as the requirements of the particular project.

PERMANENT INKS
Permanent inks, which are also available in water- and solvent-based versions, can be used on all types of papers as well as a variety of other surfaces such as tile, wood, glass, and plastic. These inks sometimes include toxic ingredients, so be sure to follow the manufacturer's instructions carefully, allow for adequate ventilation, avoid contact with eyes and skin, and protect your work surface from spatters and smears.

STAMP PADS
The purpose of a stamp pad is to hold ink so that it can be conveniently applied to a rubber stamp die. Most of the inks discussed above are available on either felt or

foam stamp pads, depending on the consistency and base of the ink's formulation. In addition to the universally recognized single-color stamp pad, rainbow stamp pads, small stamp pads, and uninked stamp pads are now widely available.

RAINBOW STAMP PADS

Rainbow pads are available in two ink types: dye-based and pigment. Generally sold in assortments of three or more colors, rainbow stamp pads come in a variety of color combinations and moods, such as primary, fantasy, spring, or holiday collections, and are a great way to acquire several colors for the price of one stamp pad.

Using a rainbow pad sometimes eliminates the need to color in an image. You can achieve wonderful colorful gradations with just one impression of your stamp, or use the individual colors within a collection to ink small stamps. Rainbow pads can also be used with a rubber brayer, sponges, or other applicators to create magnificent color backgrounds. (See "Backgrounds," pages 56–57.)

- *Dye-based ink rainbow pads* are available in two forms. One has a solid piece of felt that is hand-inked to create seamless blocks of color. The other type of dye-based rainbow pad contains separate pieces of felt with small spaces between them, which keeps colors pure. Never store dye-based rainbow pads on their sides, or the colors will bleed together and become muddy. For the best results, store them upside down, which keeps the inks close to the surface of the pads.
- *Pigment ink rainbow pads* are made with a single-piece foam pad, but the consistency of the pigment inks prevents them from bleeding into each other. To achieve a blended look when using this type of pad, move the stamp slightly in a back-and-forth motion. This prevents sharp breaks between colors.

SMALL STAMP PADS

Small stamp pads are usually about 1 inch square or oval, available in either foam or felt, and contain either dye-based or pigment inks. A quality small stamp pad is designed to have a raised surface. This allows you to ink any size stamp by picking up the stamp pad and blotting the ink onto the surface of the stamp, and to apply color to specific areas of a stamp. It is also an economical way to collect a wide variety of colors.

UNINKED STAMP PADS

Uninked stamp pads are available in both foam and felt. Felt pads are normally used with dye-based, fabric, or embossing inks, while foam pads are used with pigment or embossing inks. By adding ink to these pads, you can create any color combinations you want in a variety of shapes for distinctive color effects. For example, you can create a stamp pad specifically for stamping flowers by inking half of the pad with two shades of green and the other half with pink and red, then use a solid, broad-surface rose stamp to print several multicolor roses.

While it is possible to load an uninked stamp pad with certain "nontraditional" inks and paints, some of these materials may react to the foam or felt of the pad, or may make a pad impossible to clean and reuse with other inks.

RE-INKERS

Re-inker bottles are sold containing dye-based, pigment, embossing, fabric, and permanent inks. Typically, a re-inker has a small hole in the top through which the ink can be dispensed, either to refresh dry ink pads or ink uninked stamp pads.

STAMPING SURFACES

Just about anything can be stamped, as long as its surface is smooth and the appropriate ink is used. The following are some basic guidelines for stamping on a variety of surfaces.

PAPER

Aside from ink, paper is the most widely used element in rubber stamping projects. In fact, the paper you plan to use will dictate your choice of ink.

Currently, there's an immense proliferation of papers to choose from for creating stamped art. The popularity of handmade and recycled papers that incorporate unusual plant and cloth fibers has created a gold mine of beautiful papers. The following are just a few examples, all of which are available in a variety of colors and textures: coated and uncoated papers, handmade papers made from a variety of materials, paper lace, origami papers, rice papers, mulberry papers, kraft paper, vellum, and tissue papers. Most papers can be purchased at stationery, rubber stamp, and office or art supply and crafts stores.

There are no absolute limitations that would exclude a specific paper from being used in a project. Experimenting with papers and inks is the best way to discover which are best for your stamped art. Some papers may not be suitable for stamping but can instead be used to frame an image or as an element in a collage. Paper can also be shaped and manipulated by cutting, folding, crinkling, crimping, and layering. (See "Working with Paper," page 37.)

A representative sampling of the abundance of papers available to stampers today. Shown here are many textured, handmade, and colored stocks.

IMPORTANT CONSIDERATIONS

Your choice of paper will ultimately be determined by a review of its basic characteristics. In addition to the more obvious attributes of sheet size, weight, color, surface texture, and price, you'll need to consider the following attributes when evaluating and working with paper.

The term *absorbency* refers to a paper's capacity to accept inks and liquids. Several factors affect a paper's degree of absorbency. In addition to *density,* the compactness of a paper's fibers, and the presence of *sizing,* a material that is added to paper to provide resistance to moisture, whether a paper is coated will influence your ink choices most profoundly.

Coated papers are finished with a layer of clay, plastic, or resin, and as a result have little or no absorbency. The surface of a coated paper can be glossy, dull, or matte: Glossy coated papers have a shiny, lustrous appearance; matte coated papers have little or no shine; and dull coated papers fall somewhere in between. Either one or both sides of a sheet may be coated. Dye-based inks and water-based color markers, both of which are translucent, look particularly clear and bright on white glossy paper, but you must allow images stamped with these mediums to dry before coloring them or they will smear. Pigment inks will not dry on coated paper stock unless they are embossed. Because of their waxy consistency, colored pencils do not adhere well to glossy coated papers but can be used successfully on matte coated papers.

In contrast, *uncoated papers,* which include many fine-art as well as common household and office papers, tend to absorb inks more readily. Colored pencils, chalks, and watercolors work well with most uncoated papers. Uncoated papers can be stamped with dye-based inks and water-based markers, but their high degree of absorbency prevents the inks from looking as bright and translucent as they do on coated paper. Because pigment inks are thick and highly opaque, colors will look rich and vibrant even on colored uncoated papers.

ACID-FREE AND ARCHIVAL PAPERS

A paper's pH is measured on a scale of 1 to 14: the lower the number, the greater its acidity; the higher the number, the greater its alkalinity (a pH of 7.0 is neutral). The presence of acid in paper causes it to become brittle and fragile over time. Acid-free paper contains no harmful acid and has a pH of at least 6.5.

In order to be classified as "archival," a paper must meet national standards for permanence: It must have a pH of 7.5 to 8.5, include 2 percent calcium carbonate as an alkaline reserve, and contain no groundwood or unbleached wood fiber. Archival paper's alkalinity ensures that it won't deteriorate over time, giving it an expected life of at least 100 years.

Acid-free and archival papers are perfect for those projects you want to preserve for the future, such as photo albums and memory books. To maximize stability and improve resistance to deterioration, use pigment inks with these kinds of projects.

WOOD

The decoration of wood is a popular craft, and stamping is an easy way to embellish both unfinished and already finished wood items.

Pigment, fabric, and permanent inks all work well on wood. Since these products are manufactured by many different companies, it's always best to follow the instructions on the label. (Permanent dye-based inks and water-based markers are not recommended for use on wood, as they may transfer to your hands when the object is handled.) For coloring stamped images, use textile markers or colored pencils (*not* watercolor pencils), neither of which will smear once they're applied. Unless a glossy finish is desired or you expect that the finished product will be handled frequently, it isn't necessary to finish images stamped on wood with a glaze or sealer. When embossing on wood, use pigment ink with a translucent embossing powder or clear embossing ink with colored or metallic powder.

PREPARING UNFINISHED WOOD FOR STAMPING

Beginning with an unfinished wood item gives you the most creative freedom in planning your project, as you dictate the color and finish of the stain or paint on which the stamps will be printed. You can find a wide range of unfinished wood items at many art supply, crafts, and hardware stores, as well as at lumber yards.

If the surface of your wood item is rough, sand it until smooth, then wipe it thoroughly with a tack cloth to remove any sanding dust. To prevent the inks from bleeding into the unfinished wood, you must seal it before stamping. Unfinished wood can be embossed without prior sealing, but the powder takes longer to melt than it does on paper. If the wood grain of your piece won't compete visually with the stamps you're planning to use, you can either spray it very lightly with a matte-finish acrylic spray sealer and stamp on it as is, or brush on a coat or two of water-based stain before sealing to modify the color of the wood without obscuring its grain. Note that a heavy coat of sealer may prevent stamping ink from adhering to the surface and make it impossible to color in the image. If you prefer to stamp on a solid color, simply paint your sanded piece with a light coat of acrylic paint, which also acts as a sealant. Make sure to follow the manufacturer's instructions for application and drying times for all these products.

STAMPING ALREADY FINISHED WOOD

There are many finished wood objects that you can use as stamping projects, including frames, mirrors, storage boxes, shelves, and serving trays. While it is generally unnecessary to alter a wood finish in preparation for ink or embossing powder, the slick surfaces of glossy wood finishes are the most difficult to work with, as stamps are inclined to slip. When stamping on a glossy finish, you should "kiss" the wood with the die, using a very light touch to apply it to the surface.

Whether you stamp or emboss your finished wood piece will depend entirely on its base color. (Keep in mind that the perception of a color is always affected by the color of the background on which it appears. See "Color Fundamentals," pages 42–45.) For most light-colored projects, pigment inks are preferable to fabric and permanent inks, as they adhere to surfaces more effectively. On dark backgrounds, relief and metallic images are more striking than inked ones. As with unfinished wood, embossing on finished wood requires more time than it does on paper, and care must be taken to avoid applying heat to one area for too long a period, as it can potentially damage the finish. Move the embossing heat tool over the image continuously, and avoid applying heat to areas of the image that have already melted.

FABRICS

When stamping on fabric, smooth weaves such as muslin, cotton sheeting, and cotton T-shirts will give you the best results. (If cotton blends are used, those with higher percentages of cotton are recommended.) Although colored fabrics can be stamped, white and light colors will make inks appear more vibrant. Before stamping, always wash your fabrics to remove sizing and prevent shrinkage or bleeding the first time you wash your stamped item, then iron them carefully.

Whenever possible, use fabric inks that are specially formulated for stamping. You can also stamp fabric with pigment inks and emboss them with clear embossing powder, although the surface of the image will be slightly brittle. Outline images can be colored with textile markers, fabric paints, and acrylic paints mixed with textile medium. When coloring detailed images, use translucent fabric paints and markers so that details won't be obscured.

You can transfer (and, if desired, enlarge) a stamped image onto fabric by taking your stamped art to a copy shop that makes fabric transfers. Your image will be reproduced on a special type of paper which, when ironed, will transfer the design to the fabric. To increase accuracy of placement, you can also use fabric transfer ink to stamp your design on paper, then iron the image onto your project. Note that this method is not appropriate for word stamps, as it reverses images.

To ensure success when stamping on fabric, select stamp images with clean lines, avoiding highly detailed images. Very simple outline and solid, broad-surface rubber stamps are good choices. When stamping an image to match a coordinating fabric, select the fabric first, then match the inks to the fabric. Inks and paints can be mixed to match, whereas it is more difficult to find fabric to precisely match ink and paint colors. Before you begin, always make a few test prints on scraps of the same fabric, or on a fabric that's as similar as possible to the one you're using for your project. For maximum leverage, it's best to stand while stamping on fabric. You'll find that you may need to exert a bit more pressure than when stamping on paper. Also, the larger the stamp, the more pressure you'll need to apply.

A wide range of surfaces can be stamped, including wood, fabric, leather, terracotta, and glass.

LEATHER

If you'd like to personalize a leather photo album or garment with a stamped or embossed image, select a leather with a fairly smooth texture. (Do not stamp or emboss suede or heavily textured leather.) Use fabric inks for stamping, and textile markers to color images. To emboss on leather, use embossing powders with either embossing or pigment inks, and use extra care when applying heat to avoid damaging the surface.

TERRACOTTA

As terracotta is very porous, it must be lightly sealed with an acrylic spray sealer before stamping to prevent the ink from bleeding into it. Pigment and fabric inks can be used successfully on terracotta, and are permanent once dry. Dye-based inks should be avoided, as they will bleed into the surface of clay even after it's been sealed. If a glossy relief image is desired, use pigment inks with translucent embossing powders or embossing inks with opaque powders. While none of these materials requires sealing unless a glossy finish is desired, be aware that stamped and embossed terracotta items are purely decorative. For example, decorated terracotta tiles shouldn't be installed on floors or on surfaces that require more than an occasional cleaning with a damp sponge, and plastic liners should be used in stamped or embossed terracotta pots.

GLASS AND PORCELAIN

Available in craft, hardware, and paint stores, gloss enamel inks and acrylic enamel paints are specially formulated for stamping on glass and porcelain, on which they are permanent without firing or sealing. It should be noted that these paints won't withstand heavy traffic, abrasive cleaning, or dishwashing, and shouldn't be applied to the interiors of plates and containers used for food. Both formulations are potentially toxic, so always follow the manufacturer's instructions carefully, use with adequate ventilation, and wear gloves to avoid contact with skin. Because glass and porcelain are slick surfaces, care must be taken so that stamps won't slip or slide while making a print.

SHRINK PLASTIC™ AND CREATIVE PAPERCLAY™

Crafters of all stripes are experimenting with synthetic, plastic-based craft media. Several of these fun and versatile products can be decorated with inks and paints, making them natural surfaces for rubber stamping. The two products featured in projects in this book are Shrink Plastic and Creative Paperclay.

Sold in clear, white translucent, and white opaque sheets, Shrink Plastic can be stamped, colored, cut out, and baked to make objects such as jewelry or buttons. Use dye-based inks to stamp and water-based markers or colored pencils to color the images. When working with Shrink Plastic, keep in mind that during baking your items will be reduced to about a sixth of their original size and the colors of the stamp inks will become more intense. Several manufacturers produce Shrink Plastic, so always follow the package instructions.

In contrast, Creative Paperclay is air-dried rather than baked and remains the same size after it's dried. Roll the clay out smoothly so that the stamp image can be applied evenly. Use only pigment inks to stamp and water-based brush markers to color images. For a glossy finish, brush on an acrylic glaze or clear fingernail polish, or spray with an acrylic spray sealer. You can also use embossing inks and powders on preshaped and -dried Paperclay. Stamp the image with embossing or pigment ink, sprinkle it with embossing powder, apply heat until the powder melts, then seal with acrylic spray or glaze.

TOOLS AND SUPPLIES

In an effort to embellish and enhance their art, stampers are constantly experimenting with tools and accessories, both new and old. In the process, they've discovered unique ways of using traditional stamping tools, and developed new techniques by exploring some unconventional alternatives.

THE BASICS

You'll most probably start your inventory of supplies by purchasing a few items for your first project. As you work on other projects and investigate and develop new stamping techniques, you'll find that there are virtually no limits to what you can use. It's convenient to have most of the basic tools readily available, since they're used in most of the projects in this book.

Cutting Tools. Two cutting tools—scissors and craft knife—are indispensable in stamping projects. You'll tend to use one more than the other, depending on the kinds of projects you do as well as which feels more comfortable to you. Small scissors are great for shaping, particularly when making masks (see page 48) and cutting out stamped images. Aligning the blade of a craft knife with the edge of a metal ruler (see below) is one of the easiest and most reliable ways to cut a straight edge on a sheet of paper. Always make sure your blade is sharp so that the paper won't tear.

Rulers. A metal ruler with a cork bottom can be used as a straightedge for cutting paper with a craft knife and for drawing borders and straight lines with a marker. Because this type of ruler is raised slightly from the surface of the paper, the ink won't run under the edge and smear. A metal ruler can also be used with a bone folder (see below) as a guide for scoring paper. A transparent plastic ruler printed with a grid is useful for making precise measurements on both paper and fabric.

Cutting Mat. A self-healing cutting mat protects your work surface and preserves the sharp blade of the craft knife when cutting paper and other materials.

Blank Newsprint. Use a pad of blank newsprint to cover your work surface when stamping. In addition to protecting your table, it's great for stamping test prints, checking ink coverage, and practicing techniques. When the top sheet gets dirty, just tear it off for a quick and easy cleanup. When stamping on fabric, the newsprint works as a blotter for any ink that seeps through. When stamping on T-shirts and other wearables, insert a sheet or two inside the garment to prevent ink bleed-through.

Glues and Adhesives. Glue pens are used primarily to adhere glitters and embossing powders to paper. Their chiseled points are ideal for drawing broad or fine lines, creating borders, and handlettering. They can also be used to adhere thin sheets of paper to each other for layering and collage projects. Heavy papers, card stocks, and projects such as pop-up cards, dimensional images, and dioramas require stronger adhesives, such as glue sticks, double-stick tape, and transparent tape. Spray adhesives and other glues can also be used for these purposes, as well as for mounting art papers over card stock. Artist's tape (also referred to as low-adhesive paper tape) is used mostly for masking or as a guide for creating straight lines.

A glue gun is useful for adhering embellishments such as brass trinkets, rhinestones, raffia, and ribbon to papers. It's best to use a low-temperature glue gun and low-temperature glue, as their high-temperature counterparts can damage a paper's surface. A glue gun can also be used to adhere heavier papers in layering projects, but the glue dries quickly so you need to work fast. You can also use a glue gun to create dimension by building up a small mass of glue, then covering it lightly with a cut-out stamped image.

Foam Sponges. Sponges are used to apply inks and paints to yield a wide range of effects, from soft, airbrush-style backgrounds to solid, intense blocks of color. Sponges are also very effective for applying inks to rubber dies and over templates and masks.

The sponge used in this book is a wedge-shaped foam sponge. Many stamp companies sell sponges in various shapes, from functional wedges and discs to decorative stars and hearts, which can also be used as stamps.

Bone Folder. A bone folder is used for scoring and making sharp creases and folds in paper. The flat end of the bone folder can also be used as a burnisher, to strengthen the bond between glued papers. Before burnishing, cover the paper with tracing paper to protect its finish.

Stylus. Also effective for scoring paper, a stylus is designed to create blind embossed edges or shapes when used with a brass or cardboard template and a light table.

Embossing Heat Tool. Made specifically to melt embossing powders and puff up puff paint, an embossing heat tool emits intense heat without blowing air, which could quickly scatter powders and glitters. Its heat is quite intense, so children under the age of 12 should not use one unless supervised by an adult.

With the popularity of rubber stamping, embossing heat tools are available in many art supply and craft stores. They provide the easiest and quickest way to emboss images on a wide variety of surfaces. You can also use a hot plate, toaster oven, or an iron to melt embossing powders and glitters on paper projects. (For more information, see "Embossing," page 36.)

Basic stamping tools and supplies: rulers; blank newsprint; adhesives (a glue pen, a glue stick, adhesive tapes, and a glue gun); craft and hole punches; a cutting mat; foam dots; wedge-shaped foam sponges; a stamp positioning tool; tracing paper; a pencil; a bone folder; a small paint brush; a stylus; straight scissors; a craft knife; an eraser; Post-it™ notes; and an embossing heat tool.

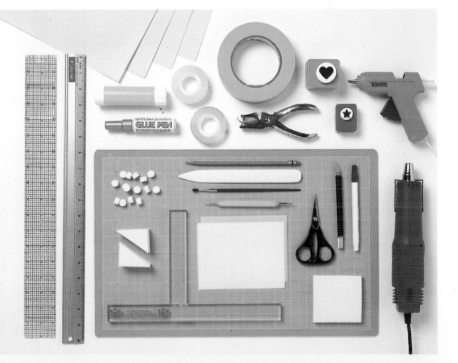

Stamp Positioning Tool. This acrylic tool is used to place images precisely where you want them, or to restamp uneven or lightly stamped images. A stamp positioning tool is also used to create straight borders by using the long side of the tool to stamp the images in a straight line, or to guide the path of a roller stamp. (See "Positioning a Stamp Accurately," pages 34–35.)

Tracing Paper and Post-it™ Notes. Tracing paper serves two important purposes in stamping. In addition to protecting the surface of paper during burnishing (see "Bone Folder," above), tracing paper is used with a stamp positioning tool to create templates of stamped images. (See "Positioning a Stamp Accurately," pages 34–35.) Post-it notes are used primarily to create masks. (See "Masking," pages 48–50.)

Hole and Craft Punches. Available in a broad range of sizes and designs, craft and hole punches are extremely versatile tools. Here are just a few ideas to help spark your imagination:

• *Create a stencil* by punching a shape or series of shapes from a scrap piece of card stock. Decorate your project by coloring the stencil with an inked sponge.
• *Make stickers* by punching shapes out of sticker paper.
• *Punch a novelty shape* through the corner of a gift tag, then thread it with ribbon or twine and attach it to a gift.

COLOR ACCESSORIES

Color is an exciting element of rubber stamping, and the color media available to stampers provide a wide range of color choices, from the highly saturated colors of brush markers to the soft, velvety colors of colored pencils. While most of the media listed below are used to add color to stamped outline prints, others, like brush markers, can also be used to ink a rubber die. For more information on choosing and using colors, see "Color Fundamentals," pages 42–45, and "Working with Color," pages 46–47.

Brush Markers. Brush markers can be used to color in an outline image "coloring book" style, or to apply color directly to the rubber die, both for single-color and blended effects. Many types of brush markers are available in a variety of tip-widths, from broad to fine as well as double-ended. Several brands of brush markers are manufactured specifically for rubber stamping, including Marvy, Pigma Sumi, Tombow, Staedtler, and Zig. They all contain water-based inks that can be cleaned from rubber dies and used on all types of papers. Although their colors are initially very intense, images stamped with water-based markers will fade over time.

Permanent markers should be used *only* to color in stamped images, but should *not* be used to ink rubber stamps, as their inks will be absorbed by the rubber dies and contaminate any colors used afterward. In contrast to water-based markers, the colors of permanent markers are resistant to fading.

Colored Pencils. If you like soft, subtle color, or if the colors of brush markers are too intense for a particular project, colored pencils are a good choice for coloring your stamped images. They work particularly well with natural, romantic, and Victorian-style images. Except for glossy coated papers, colored pencils can be used on most paper stocks and other matte-finish surfaces.

Watercolors. Widely available in three forms—cakes, tubes, and pencils (see opposite)—watercolor can be used with stamped images in a number of ways. Backgrounds stroked with a gentle wash of watercolor, watercolor compositions enhanced with patterns of stamped images, and outline stamps carefully tinged with watercolor are some of the ways these media can be combined.

If you want to color a stamped image with watercolor, you must first emboss it with pigment or clear embossing ink and embossing powder to prevent it from running. However, if you avoid touching the outline of the stamped image with the wet brush, it is possible to add watercolor images stamped in dye-based and pigment inks even if they aren't embossed. Select a large stamp with simple lines and few details if you wish to use watercolors in this manner.

Watercolor Pencils. Watercolor pencils look like regular colored pencils and can be used dry for the same results. But when dipped in water or stroked with a wet brush, they act just like tube or pan watercolors. In fact, watercolor pencils are more appropriate than traditional watercolors for adding color to stamped, unembossed images, since they can be used dry to color a portion of an image, then stroked with a moist brush to carefully move the color within its contours.

Chalks. In addition to colored pencils, chalks provide stampers with subtle, delicate color. In fact, their working properties are very similar, as chalks are also blended by means of layering. Chalks can be applied directly to paper, to which this dusty medium is best suited. Apply chalk to wood with a cotton swab or your finger, then add a finishing layer of fixative to protect the image and prevent it from disintegrating. Do not use chalks on fabric.

A variety of tools for adding color and texture: fine-point and brush markers; colored pencils; embossing powders and glitters; watercolors in pans, pencils, and tubes; novelty-edge scissors; a rubber brayer; foam sponges; calligraphy pens; a tube wringer; trinket embellishments; puff paint; glitter glue pens; and textile markers.

STAMPING TECHNIQUES

The preceding chapter surveys the profusion of materials and supplies that can be used in rubber stamping. In this chapter, we look at *how* these materials are used, from the relatively simple procedure of inking a stamp, to cutting, folding, and tearing paper; from combining stamped images to suggest depth or motion, to devising beautiful backgrounds, borders, and edges to complement your stamp art. Several approaches to designing a stamped surface are also covered, as well as how to choose and use color effectively. While these basic techniques and methods are essential for creating impressive projects, they represent only a fraction of those you can use to create stamped art. Experimentation is the key to success in rubber stamping. Don't be afraid to try something new, to imagine new possibilities.

INKING A STAMP

TIPS FOR STAMPING SUCCESS

- It's best to work on a smooth, flat, hard surface. To protect your work surface from ink blotches and smudges, cover it with several layers of blank newsprint.
- Before inking, make sure the die is dry and free of any ink, dust, or glitter. Use a piece of tape to remove any stubborn debris.
- Check the die before stamping to make sure the entire image is inked.
- Stamp the surface by applying firm pressure. Do *not* wiggle or rock the stamp, or the print will blur. The larger the stamp, the more pressure you'll need to apply to make a clear, evenly stamped print.
- After making your print, lift the stamp straight up while holding down a corner of the surface. This ensures that the print won't blur or smear as you remove the stamp.

Although the basic procedure for inking a stamp with a traditional felt stamp pad seems fairly obvious—pressing the rubber die to the pad, then printing on the intended surface—there are a few important guidelines to follow to ensure that the stamp is inked evenly and its print is clean and clear. In addition, the basic procedure reflects only a limited notion of the ever-widening variety of materials now used in this inventive craft. By using brush markers to apply color directly to the rubber die, for example, you can stamp a multicolored image in a single print, or increase the versatility of your images by inking only part of a stamp.

INKING WITH ONE-COLOR STAMP PADS

When inking a stamp with a stamp pad, you must consider the type of pad you're using. The surface of a felt pad is relatively hard, and thus requires an additional touch of pressure during inking. Foam pads, in contrast, are softer, so avoid applying too much pressure as you ink the stamp, or the coverage on the die may be excessive, particularly in the crevices. In any case, overinking affects the quality of your print.

The stamp pad's raised surface enables you to ink a large rubber stamp that's longer or wider than the pad. Simply tap the stamp over the entire surface of the pad, lifting and moving it until all areas of the die are inked. Another method is to pick up the stamp pad and tap it directly onto the rubber die.

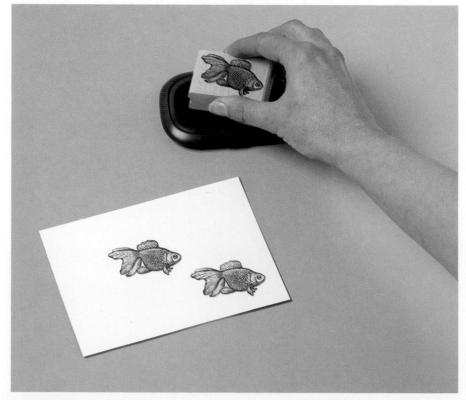

When inking with a foam stamp pad, use a light touch to avoid overinking. Apply slightly more pressure on a felt pad, which is somewhat harder than a foam one.

INKING WITH RAINBOW STAMP PADS

It's easy to achieve wonderful color-gradated prints with rainbow stamp pads. Simply ink the stamp on the pad and stamp it on your surface. The arrangement of colors on the stamp pad will be reflected in the print.

The colors of some dye-based rainbow stamp pads are on individual pieces of felt with small spaces in between, to keep the colors from bleeding into each other. Pigment ink rainbow pads are made with foam, but the thick consistency of the ink prevents the colors from intermixing. To avoid printing sharp breaks or gaps between colors, move the rubber stamp back and forth slightly over the pad until the entire surface of the die is inked.

INKING WITH BRUSH MARKERS

Inking a stamp with brush markers allows you to apply a different color to each area of a stamp, creating a beautiful multicolor image with just one impression. This technique is particularly useful in achieving color gradations, blends, and watercolor looks. (See "Blending Color," page 47.) You can use brush markers to ink any type of stamp, and many broad-surface stamps are specifically designed to be inked with brush markers. Although you can use permanent markers to color stamped prints, use only water-based brush markers to ink the rubber dies of your stamps. Permanent marker inks are absorbed by the rubber and will contaminate any colors you use afterward.

Another effective brush marker technique is that of isolating part of a stamp design by inking only a specific portion of it. You can stamp several distinct images using one complex stamp with this technique. For example, you can ink just a single flower of a sunflowers stamp, then stamp it several times to create a border (as shown below, right), or ink only the leaves to stamp a background of foliage for another stamp.

After you color a die with markers, moisten any inks that may have begun to dry by puffing warm, moist air on the die before stamping. For the cleanest, brightest prints, stamp on glossy coated white paper.

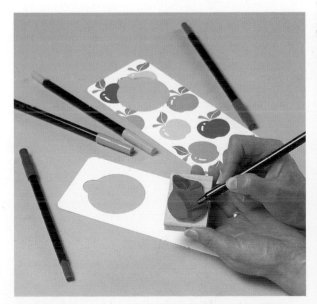

Brush markers can be used to ink specific areas of a rubber stamp die. Broad-surface stamps work particularly well with brush markers.

Increase the versatility of your stamps by using brush markers to isolate part of a stamped image.

POSITIONING A STAMP ACCURATELY

By using a stamp positioning tool, an alignment tool made specifically for stamping, you can stamp your prints precisely where you want them. Typically made of clear, heavy acrylic, a stamp positioning tool looks like either an L-square or a T-square, except that the horizontal part is longer than the vertical. Some are even attached to a grid printed on a block of wood.

The basic technique requires a template of the stamped image. To make a template, you'll need a piece of tracing paper that's large enough to accommodate the image. Place a corner of the piece of tracing paper in a right-angle corner of the stamp positioning tool, then stamp the image by aligning the corner of its block within the same right angle. You can then move the tracing paper template to wherever you're planning to stamp the image, align the right-angle corner of the positioning tool with the corner of the template, remove the template, then stamp the image by aligning the corner of the block with the corner of the tool. (In the example shown on the opposite page, a corner stamp was used to create a square border, so both the template and the stamp positioning tool were positioned four times, starting with the top left-hand corner of the border.) A stamp positioning tool can also be used to position a mask when combining images or composing landscapes (see page 50), or to restamp a poorly or unevenly inked image.

You can use the long side of a stamp positioning tool to create accurate borders, either by aligning an individual stamp's base against it to keep all the prints straight, or by using it to guide the path of a roller stamp.

MAKING CORRECTIONS

There will be times when you'll need to correct a bad print or remove ink smudges. Try some of these correction techniques:

- *Redo it.* Use a stamp positioning tool to restamp a weak or uneven print. Align the template over the misprint, ink the stamp evenly, remove the template, and align the corner of the stamp's block with the corner of the stamp positioning tool.
- *Take it off.* Many ink smudges can be easily removed with a Staedtler eraser. If you're working on glossy paper, you can use a craft knife to gently scrape off any smudges or bad prints after they've dried.
- *Cover it up.* Restamp the image on sticker paper, cut it out, and place it over the mistake. For a dimensional look, restamp the image on another piece of paper or card stock, cut it out, and layer it over the bad print with foam tape or dots. Correction fluid can be also used to cover up mistakes—just make sure that its color is as close to the paper's as possible.
- *Camouflage it.* Collage is a great way to conceal mistakes. Use bits of recycled paper, magazine clippings, and other found treasures to cover misprints. (If all else fails, you can always cut the misprint into shapes and use it in another stamping project or collage.) You can also hide a misprint beneath smaller stamped images, such as stars or hearts. Another way to camouflage smudges or misprints is to conceal them with hand-drawn embellishments made with a fine-point marker, including mini dot trios, squiggles, or multiple lines.

1. Place a corner of a piece of tracing paper in a right-angle corner of the stamp positioning tool, then ink and stamp the image, carefully aligning the edges of the block with the corner of the tool.

2. The image that results will serve as a template for positioning.

3. Position the tracing paper template wherever you wish to stamp the image, then align the corner of the positioning tool with the corner of the template.

4. Remove the template, then guide the inked stamp into the corner of the tool as explained in step 1.

5. The stamped print will be precisely where you had placed its tracing paper template.

6. To create a square border with this corner stamp, the template and the stamp positioning tool were repositioned so that the corner of the tool that had originally been used to create the template was the same for each print.

7. The completed border, colored with colored pencils.

1

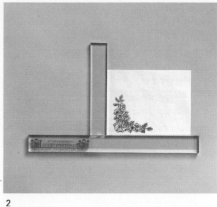
2

3

4

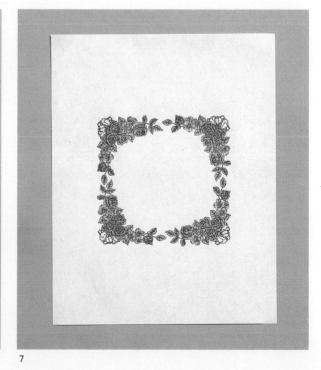
5

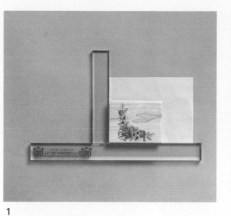
6

7

35

EMBOSSING

Thermal embossing uses slow-drying ink, embossing powder, and a heat source to create a lustrous, raised image. The image is printed with either pigment or embossing ink, then sprinkled with embossing powder. Heat is applied to melt the powder so that it bonds with the ink and adheres to the stamping surface.

If you use embossing ink, which is clear, use an opaque embossing powder. When using pigment ink, select a translucent embossing powder so that the color of the ink will show through. If you use an opaque powder over pigment ink, the embossed image will be the same color as the powder. You can make glittery embossing powders by combining fine glitter with embossing powder, as long as the mixture includes at least 75 percent embossing powder.

After printing the image with embossing or pigment ink and sprinkling it with embossing powder, tap the surface over a sheet of paper, then remove any remaining stray flecks with a clean paint brush. Use the sheet of paper to return the excess powder to the original container. When embossing on paper and fabric, apply heat with an embossing heat tool by holding it approximately 1 inch over the image, moving it from one small area to the next as the powder melts. In addition to an embossing heat tool, you can use the following appliances to melt embossing powders on paper, though care must be taken to avoid burning the paper:

- *Hot plate or toaster oven.* Hold the paper with long tweezers and position the embossed image over the heat source until the powder melts.
- *Iron.* Heat the iron to its medium-temperature setting, then place the unembossed side of the paper against the base until the powder on the other side melts.

With the notable exception of glass, which is too fragile to endure the heat required to melt embossing powder, stamp images can be embossed on practically any surface. It's recommended, however, that you emboss test prints on every new surface to make sure that it won't be damaged by the heat of the embossing tool. (For embossing guidelines for other surfaces, see pages 20–21 and 23.)

1. Stamp the image with embossing (clear) or pigment (opaque) ink, then sprinkle it generously with embossing powder. (Use opaque powders with embossing ink, and transparent embossing powders with pigment inks.) The powder will cling to the areas that were stamped.
2. Tap all excess powder off the image onto a separate sheet of paper.
3. If necessary, use a small clean paint brush to remove any stray flecks of powder. Flex the separate sheet of paper into a funnel shape and use it to return the excess powder to the original container.
4. Apply heat with an embossing heat tool until the powder melts.

1

2

3

4

WORKING WITH PAPER

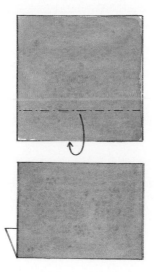

An example of a valley fold (top) and a mountain fold (bottom).

Paper can be shaped and manipulated by means of cutting, folding, and tearing. Although ready-made papers made specifically for stamping are now available, paper-shaping skills give stampers greater creative latitude.

CUTTING

Paper can be cut and shaped with either a scissors or a craft knife. Scissors come in various sizes, with both straight and decorative blades. To make detailed cutouts, use small or cuticle scissors. Move the paper instead of the scissors to achieve smooth curves, and use the points to cut into corners to create sharp outlines. To cut a continuous edge with decorative-blade scissors, begin cutting into the paper, realign the blades against the end of the cut edge, then repeat.

When cutting with a craft knife, protect your work surface (and the blade of the knife) with a self-healing cutting mat. Make sure the blade is very sharp or it will tear the paper rather than cut it. Use a metal ruler as a guide for cutting straight edges.

FOLDING

Most papers have a *grain,* which is the predominant direction of the arrangement of its fibers. While machine-made papers all have a pronounced grain, handmade papers do not, as their fibers are randomly distributed throughout each sheet.

Grain is an important factor in folding paper. When paper is folded with the grain it bends quite easily and the fold will have a clean edge, but if it is folded against the grain it is difficult to crease, the fold will be rough and broken, and the surface of the paper may even crack, especially if it is coated. To determine the direction of the grain, gently bend the sheet of paper in half, first horizontally, then vertically, without creasing. It will flex more easily with the grain. Since handmade papers don't have a grain, they're generally easier to fold than machine-made papers, although heavy handmade papers as well as those that contain long or hard fibers are a bit more difficult to tear. (See "Tearing," below.)

The two basic types of folds are *valley* and *mountain folds.* These terms refer to the orientation of the fold—that is, the side of the fold that should be facing you—during the construction of a project. Paper can be folded and creased by hand, but if you prefer a sharper fold, cover the paper with scrap or tissue paper and run the flat edge of a bone folder along the edge of the crease.

When folding heavy papers, it may be helpful to score the fold first. Place a metal ruler along the line of the fold, then use a stylus, the pointed edge of a bone folder, or the dull edge of a craft knife to lightly score a line against its edge. Crease and fold the paper along the scored line. Always score on the outer side of the fold.

TEARING

Papers also tear more easily along the grain, leaving a smooth edge, whereas tearing against the grain will create a ragged, uneven edge. To make a straight tear, align a metal ruler with the grain of the paper at the tear line, then pull up on the paper while pressing down on the ruler.

To create deckle edges, which are the natural, fuzzy edges seen on handmade papers, use the wet-and-tear method. Fold the paper along the tear line, then dampen the fold with a paint brush moistened with water. Allow the water to penetrate the paper, then pull the paper apart at the fold.

DESIGN STRATEGIES

The truly creative part of rubber stamping lies in the selection and combination of elements for each particular project—whether one image or several are used, their number and arrangement, and the colors they're stamped in, as well as the color and visual texture of the stamping surface. All of these choices are purely individual, limited only by the imagination of the stamper.

GATHERING IDEAS

Everyone needs a starting point, and sometimes you'll find inspiration where you least expect it. Below are some methods used by artists and designers to compile a creative visual inventory for their projects:

- *Be observant.* Note the diversity of color and texture in nature: the many blues in the sky, and the multitude of greens in the foliage in your garden. Your heightened sense of observation will enliven your art.
- *Keep a sketchbook or journal.* Carry it with you wherever you go, and use it to jot down ideas and sketch or describe scenes, objects, and color combinations you find interesting.
- *Start a clip file.* Collect anything that appeals to you. I save magazine clippings, greeting cards, photographs, swatches of fabric, gift wrap, postcards, and pages from catalogs and old calendars. As your collection grows, you can categorize your reference materials into file folders, organizing them by subject, color, or some other arrangement.
- *Start a library.* Clear a space on your bookshelf for reference books and magazines on subjects that you find visually inspiring. Photography, crafts, painting, interior design, and architecture are just a few possibilities.

COMPOSING A LAYOUT

Regardless of the project you're working on, you'll find it helpful to stamp the images on scrap paper, cut them out, and arrange them on the stamping surface, experimenting with several arrangements so you can visualize what each will look like before you actually begin stamping. You can also use this technique to explore color combinations. Once you're pleased with the layout, you'll need to determine which images should be stamped first, which need to be masked, how to stamp the images efficiently, and the tools that are required to achieve the final layout. The layouts for most of the projects in this book were completed as follows:

1. All of the images were stamped on scrap paper, cut out, and arranged on the stamping surface to create a pleasing design.
2. The stamped scrap paper version of each image was removed and the image was stamped in its place. The images were either stamped directly on the project, or placed precisely by using a stamp positioning tool as follows:
   - A tracing paper template for each stamp image was prepared (see pages 34–35).
   - The template was then placed exactly over the scrap paper version within the layout, and the stamp positioning tool was aligned with the template.
   - Both the template and the scrap paper were removed, leaving the stamp positioning tool in place. The image was then stamped, using the positioning tool as a guide for alignment.

The spacing between elements is as important as the elements themselves in creating a pleasing and balanced layout.

WORKING WITHIN SPECIFIC PARAMETERS

There are many ways to approach the design of a project, and you can arrive at a strategy from several different angles. Sometimes the object or surface you're working on will help define your approach. For example, you might be inspired to use a single image to create a focal point on a wooden tray or jewelry box; repeat the same image at regular intervals to make an allover pattern for gift wrap; print it several times in a single row to embellish a piece of stationery. If you're stamping a border on a picture frame, you must calculate the number of images you'll need to stamp around the frame, as well as the amount of space to leave between images so that the completed design looks balanced. Your project may be a pillow, an apron, or a wooden tray, all of which come in different sizes and shapes. Here are some tips for creating effective designs within specific parameters:

- *For squares and rectangles,* start by placing images at each corner, then position other images along the borders. Begin each border by placing an image at the center, then adjust the spacing of the other images so that the borders look balanced. You may find it necessary to incorporate stamps in other sizes—both smaller and larger—for this approach to work.
- *For circles,* lightly draw a circle in the desired size. (If necessary, use a compass or template as a guide.) Place images at noon, three, six, and nine o'clock positions. Balance images equally within each quarter.
- *For borders on T-shirts and other wearables,* begin by placing an image at the center of the garment, then position the first and last images in the row. Build up your pattern until the border is complete. Adjust the spacing between images as needed so that the border fits comfortably within your garment's dimensions.

Occasionally, you will find that your design ideas won't conform readily to the shape of the object or surface you're planning to stamp, and may require some additional planning. For instance, the approach to laying out a randomly stamped allover print for a T-shirt will differ greatly from one for a highly structured border design.

CREATING PATTERNS

Creating patterns is probably one of the most interesting ways to play with stamps. The variety of borders and designs you can make with even one stamp is practically limitless. Here are a few guidelines for pattern formation:

- *Spacing.* Variations in spacing between stamped elements will dramatically affect the look of your pattern. Sometimes the spaces between elements can become the focal point of a design.
- *Rotating.* Numerous stamp patterns can be achieved by changing the orientation of your stamp. Experiment by positioning the images upside down, sideways, and at various angles.

The orientation of a stamp can be modified to produce a variety of patterns.

- *Circular patterns.* These can be achieved by pivoting a single image around a central point or by drawing a circular pattern as a guide.
- *Grouping.* Several individual designs can be grouped together to form larger ones. Experiment by combining large and small images. The contrast between them will create visual interest.

REPEATS

A *repeat* is a pattern whose elements occur in a continuous flow, at regular intervals and without interruption. Although some patterns may at first appear to be randomly designed, it's possible that their repeats are just too complex to discern. There are two basic types of repeat patterns: square and half-drop.

- A *square repeat* is laid out so that each unit of the design matches up with the side of the next one, to create a continuous pattern both vertically and horizontally. The pattern can be made up of a single design element or a combination of several different ones, and can be any shape or size, as long as the repeat structure is constant. Also, the dimensions of a design unit in a square repeat don't necessarily have to be equal in length and width: Any rectangular repeat can be considered a square repeat.

Create a circular pattern by rotating a single image around a central point (right). When combining images in a larger composition, begin by drawing a circular pattern as a guide (far right).

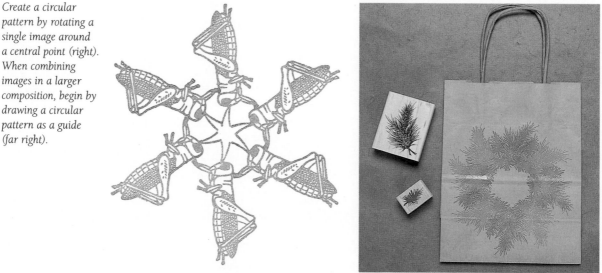

By repeating an image and varying its orientation, you can make an unusual border (left) or a distinct pattern (right).

Combine smaller images—in this example, several geometric shapes— to create a larger design.

These patterns are basic examples of the two types of repeats: square (right) and half-drop (far right).

- A *half-drop repeat* is laid out following the same basic principle, except that adjacent design units are dropped halfway down the length of the overall pattern. Half-drop repeats can also be oriented horizontally instead of vertically. Some interesting diagonal effects can be achieved by dropping adjacent design units anywhere along the length or width of the first design unit.

Use the examples above as basic guides to creating your own repeat patterns. Keep in mind that you can use more than one stamp image to create a repeat pattern, as long as the elements within a unit of design are used consistently. Look for inspiration in the many fabrics and surfaces in your home, including clothing, draperies, wallpapers, and domestic linens, that are printed with complex repeat patterns.

COMPOSING A LANDSCAPE OR SCENE

The rules for creating landscapes and scenes are derived from the basic principles of perspective. Objects that are closer to the viewer appear larger, while more distant objects appear smaller. To create an effective scene, pay particular attention to the relative sizes of your rubber stamp images, and keep in mind that the bottom of your paper appears closest to the viewer. Start off by stamping your foreground images first, then mask them as you work your way back within the scene. (See "Combining Images in a Single Scene," page 50.)

Color relationships are as important as those of size in portraying a realistic landscape. In general, bright, intense, and warm colors tend to advance, or move toward the viewer, within a composition, while dark, dull, and cool colors tend to recede. To express distance, colors should become gradually less intense as they recede. You should also think about how light within a scene affects its colors. Consider the direction of the sunlight and the areas it will illuminate within the scene, as well as those that would be shadowed. (See "Color Fundamentals," pages 42–45; and "Shadows," page 51.)

THE PRINCIPAL ELEMENTS OF COMPOSITION
- *Focus.* Establish a focal point or main element, then balance it with other elements.
- *Direction.* Create a path of vision that leads the viewer's eye to the focal point.
- *Balance.* Establish balance among the sizes, colors, values, and relationships of design elements.

COLOR FUNDAMENTALS

Color is an integral and exciting part of rubber stamping. For some people, deciding which colors to stamp with is merely a matter of using their personal favorites, regardless of the project. For many others, however, making good color choices can be difficult and confusing. In most cases, the image you'll be stamping and its intended application will help you sort things out.

For instance, if you're making a pillow that you'll display in your home, the image you select and colors you choose should coordinate with the decor and color scheme of a particular room. Sometimes the theme of a project suggests color choices. For example, soft, muted colors work best for romantic looks; warm earth tones and rich greens and blues are a good bet for nature-inspired projects; and modern designs seem to call for bold, metallic, and glittery colors. Regardless of which colors you prefer to use, an understanding of color theory is essential for making color work in all your stamped creations. Every color can be described in terms of four properties: hue, value, intensity, and temperature.

- *Hue*—which is also another word for color—is the characteristic of a color that designates it as red, yellow, blue, and so on. For example, the hue of ochre is yellow-orange; the hue of turquoise is blue-green.
- *Value* refers to the relative lightness or darkness of a color, as it relates to white, black, or the range of grays in between. A color can be described as light, medium, or dark in value. For example, yellow is light in value; violet is dark in value. A color's value can be changed by mixing it with white, black, or gray. A *tint* is made by mixing a color with white; a *tone* is made by mixing a color with gray; and a *shade* is made by mixing a color with black.
- *Intensity*—also known as *saturation* or *chroma*—refers to the relative brightness or dullness of a color. Pure colors—those that remain untainted by any others— are the highest in intensity. The primary colors (see below) are the purest on the color wheel. The secondary colors are less intense because they are mixtures.
- *Temperature* is a somewhat subjective appraisal of a color. Colors are seen as either warm or cool, primarily as a result of our associations of color in nature. Reds, oranges, and yellows are associated with warmth because of fire and the sun. Blues, greens, and purples are considered cool because of the coolness of the sky, space, and the sea.

THE COLOR WHEEL

When light is refracted through a prism, the *spectrum,* a sequence of distinct bands of pure color, can be observed. A *color wheel* is a circular arrangement of the spectrum that illustrates the relationships among the three *primary colors*— yellow, red, and blue—whose positions create an equilateral triangle within the color wheel. All other colors are created from a mixture of these three colors. Each of the three *secondary colors* is a mixture of two of the primaries: yellow + red = orange; red + blue = violet; and blue + yellow = green. The six *tertiary colors* are made by mixing a primary color with an adjacent secondary; for example, red + orange = red-orange; yellow + green = yellow-green.

Excluded from the color wheel are black, white, and the range of grays in between. These are referred to as *achromatic colors,* which simply means that they contain no color at all.

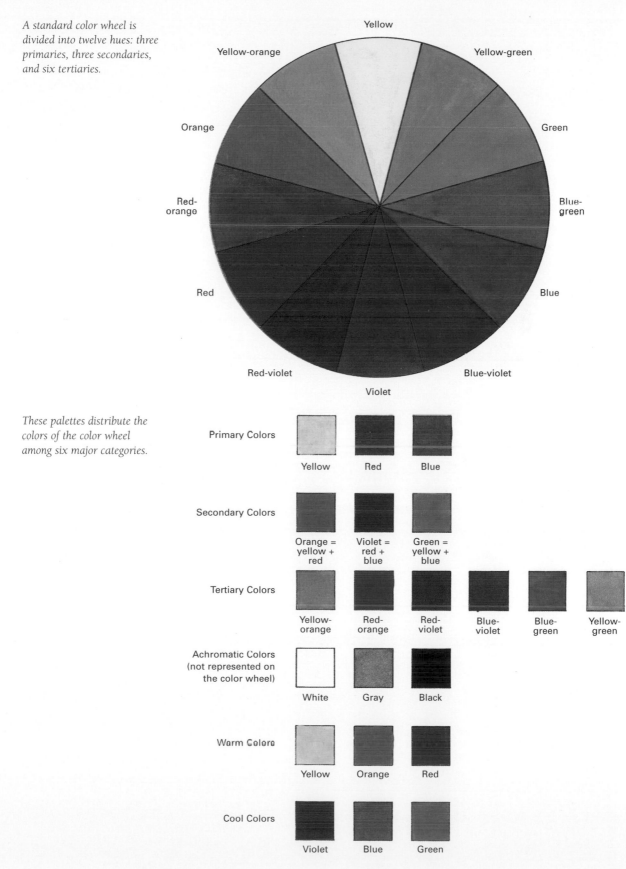

A standard color wheel is divided into twelve hues: three primaries, three secondaries, and six tertiaries.

Yellow

Yellow-green

Green

Blue-green

Blue

Blue-violet

Violet

Red-violet

Red

Red-orange

Orange

Yellow-orange

These palettes distribute the colors of the color wheel among six major categories.

Primary Colors

Yellow Red Blue

Secondary Colors

Orange = yellow + red

Violet = red + blue

Green = yellow + blue

Tertiary Colors

Yellow-orange

Red-orange

Red-violet

Blue-violet

Blue-green

Yellow-green

Achromatic Colors (not represented on the color wheel)

White Gray Black

Warm Colors

Yellow Orange Red

Cool Colors

Violet Blue Green

43

COLOR AND PERCEPTION

All color is perceived within the context of various forms of contrast, which can be manipulated to guide the eye of the viewer through a composition.

- *Contrasts of hue.* The most vivid contrast of hue occurs between two *complementary colors,* which lie directly opposite one another on the color wheel. For example, red and green are complements, as are orange and blue.
- *Contrasts of value.* Dark or low-value colors are perceived to be heavier in weight than light or high-value colors. High-value colors appear to expand space, while low-value colors appear to compress it. A color outlined with black or a low-value color looks more saturated than when it is outlined in white or a color of higher value. Movement and distance can be expressed by gradually increasing the value of a color from dark to light.
- *Contrasts of intensity.* A color of medium intensity appears dull when compared to a pure hue, but will appear brighter when compared to a low-intensity color.
- *Contrasts of temperature.* Warm colors tend to advance or move toward the viewer within a composition, while cool colors tend to recede. To enhance perspective within a composition, use warmer colors in the foreground and cooler ones in the background. Cool colors expand space, while warm colors tend to compress it.
- *Contrasts of extent.* Colors appear more intense when applied to a large area. A large area of color influences the appearance of any colors that lie within it. For example, colors appear lighter within a dark or low-value background, and appear darker within a light or high-value background.

It's important to note that factors such as the quality of the light by which we view an object and the color and texture of the background or surface on which a color appears also affect our perception of color.

COLOR SCHEMES

A *color scheme* (also referred to as a *color harmony, color chord,* or *palette)* is a group of colors used in a composition.

- *Monochromatic color schemes* use just one hue in a range of tints, shades, and tones. To create visual interest and prevent monotony, apply the colors in a variety of textures and finishes. For example, you could use metallic gray with other shades of gray, or perhaps with puff paint or silver glitter to add textural interest.
- *Analogous color schemes* include two to five colors adjacent to each other on the color wheel. Analogous colors make the most harmonious palettes because they all share a common color. The color scheme of blue, green, and green-blue—a primary, a secondary, and a tertiary color—is an analogous palette.
- *Complementary color schemes* consist of two colors that lie directly opposite one another on the color wheel. Each pair of complements includes a warm and a cool color.
- *Split-complementary color schemes* include a color from one side of the color wheel and the two colors on either side of its complement. The grouping green, red-orange, and violet-red is an example of a split-complementary palette.
- *Triadic color schemes* use three colors that are equidistant from one another on the color wheel. One example of a triadic color combination would be red, yellow, and blue; another would be green, violet, and orange.
- *Tetradic color schemes* include four colors, which are always two sets of complements. These combinations are created by placing a square or rectangle over the color wheel and rotating it to yield different groups of colors.

COLOR IN PRACTICE

One way to illustrate color relationships and the ways in which they affect perception is to compare different color schemes by using them in similar compositions.

- *To create an illusion of depth within a landscape,* stamp darker shades in the foreground and progressively lighter ones as you work toward the background. Variations in color and value can be achieved either by using several shades of a single color, or by inking a stamp once and repeatedly stamping the image without re-inking for a fade-out effect. Both methods were used in all four examples on this page.

- *Don't underestimate the visual possibilities of color temperature for attracting the viewer's attention.* In the example below, left, the coolness of the blues and greens is relieved only by the warmth of the brown tree trunks in the mid- to foreground, which leads the eye into the image and emphasizes the reflections in the immediate foreground. In the landscape below, right, the coolness of the dark green of the foreground trees is underscored not only by the warmth of the soft ochre earth and tree trunks, but by the extremely yellowed green that was used to stamp some of the trees toward the background. In the scene bottom, left, the cool blues and neutral grays of the trees are set off by a soft red-violet at the top of the composition. A pale blue was used to create a transition between the two bands of temperature.

- *Use complements to provoke contrast.* The pure visual power of the scene bottom, right, lies in its use of complements: various greens of the foliage contrasting with the bright, intense reds and oranges of the sky. Complementary colors are mutually intensifying, resulting in the greatest color vibration. In fact, when used carelessly, complementary contrast can become visually overpowering. The contrast within the example was softened by using a yellowed green for the background trees, and a light orange where those trees meet the sky.

(Right) This wintry scene was stamped with cool blues and greens. To create the reflections in the foreground, the trees were stamped upside down in the coolest shades of blue. (Far right) The contrast in this scene is one of temperature: cool color (dark green trees) set off against warm color (tree trunks, foreground clearing, and background trees).

(Right) This cool, dark nightscape is set off by the warmth of a violet sky. (Far right) The intensity of the brilliant sunset in this scene is heightened by the complementary contrast between the reds of the sky and the greens of the trees.

WORKING WITH COLOR

As useful as a knowledge of color theory can be, the application of that knowledge must take into account the characteristics and limitations of the materials you use.

ADDING COLOR TO A STAMPED IMAGE

Coloring with Brush Markers. Water-based brush markers can be used to color images stamped with dye-based and pigment inks and embossed with embossing powders. Use bright, transparent colors so that the details of the stamped image will show through. Solvent-based permanent markers also work well with the same kinds of inks. When preparing an archival project, stamp images with pigment inks and color them with permanent markers, as both are resistant to fading.

Coloring with Colored Pencils. Colored pencils also work well with both dye-based and pigment inks. By building up color in layers, you can achieve subtle color blends and variations. Use a white pencil to add highlights or tone colors down.

The raised detailing on embossed images makes it difficult to achieve smooth color application with colored pencils, but colored pencils can be used if the image doesn't contain a great deal of stippling or shading.

Coloring with Watercolors. Watercolors work best with embossed images. The embossing acts as a resist, so that color can be applied without distorting or smearing the stamped image. Images stamped with fabric inks can also be painted with watercolor without smearing. Both dye-based and pigment inks will smear if they're painted directly with watercolor. Simple outline stamps can be successfully painted with watercolor if care is taken to avoid the ink. When done intentionally, however, some interesting color-wash effects can be achieved.

Watercolor pencils are an extremely flexible form of watercolor. They can be used dry to color a portion of a stamped image, then stroked with a wet paint brush to pull the color through other areas of the image, resulting in a soft, gradient effect. A watercolor pencil can also be dipped into water before drawing, or used to draw on dampened paper. In addition, a wet brush can be loaded with color by stroking it against the lead of a watercolor pencil. You can also use a scrap piece of watercolor paper as a palette. Color a small area with the watercolor pencil, then moisten with a wet paint brush to draw color into it. Use a very wet brush for lighter, softer color, and a drier one for more intense color.

When working with watercolor, the choice of paper requires special attention. Some watercolor papers (those categorized as "rough" and "cold-pressed") are highly textured and will affect the quality of your stamped image. Thin papers must also be avoided, as they tend to buckle when wet. You can minimize buckling by stretching the paper (see page 75). If you're stamping over watercolor, make sure the surface is completely dry before you proceed.

Coloring with Foam Sponges. Apply color to a wedge sponge by rolling the tip of a brush marker against its flat edge or by dabbing it on a stamp pad. Avoid inking its edges, or clearly defined lines of color will be left on the stamping surface. Use a separate sponge for each color.

BLENDING COLOR

Blending Color with Brush Markers. Apply color directly to the rubber die, starting with the lightest. You can use this color to highlight specific portions of the image, or to cover its entire surface. Then apply the next lightest color, overlapping a portion of the first. To achieve a gradual blend from a light color to a dark one, or between two contrasting or harmonizing colors, apply the lighter hue at the point where they meet to subtly blend the two together. (If you prefer distinct lines of demarcation between colors, eliminate this step.) If the tip of your brush marker picks up any of the darker ink, clean it by rolling the tip on a paper towel until its ink is pure.

Blending Color with Stamp Pads. Both single-color and rainbow stamp pads can be used to create impressive color blends. You can use two single-color pads to ink a stamp image, much as you would with two brush markers. Begin by inking the entire die with the lighter color, then carefully stamp part of it onto a darker ink pad before stamping your project. To avoid contaminating the darker ink, wipe off any of the lighter color that remains on the darker pad. Small stamp pads with raised surfaces are particularly useful for color blending.

When blending colors with a rainbow stamp pad, first consider which of its colors you want on your image, then ink the stamp on the corresponding areas of the pad. To create a subtle, blended spectrum, gently tap the die slightly back and forth across the pad to mix the colors.

Blending Color with Foam Sponges. Apply ink to the flat edge of the sponge with either an ink pad or a brush marker, then dab the color onto the stamp. Begin by applying the lightest color first, working through the rest of the palette from next lightest to darkest. Blend colors by overlapping the darker shades with lighter ones.

Blending Color with Embossing Powders. Ink and stamp the image with embossing or pigment ink, then carefully sprinkle embossing powder on specific areas of the image. Tap off the excess. Sprinkle powder in a contrasting or complementary color on the rest of the image, then tap off the excess and use an embossing heat tool to melt the powder.

This recipe card and matching kitchen magnet illustrate the beauty of color blending with brush markers. Some of the images were inked with as many as six different colors.

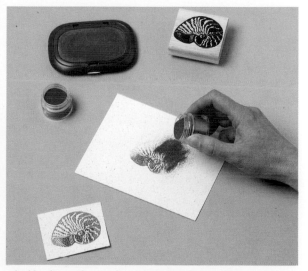

The blending technique for embossing powders allows you to achieve unusual combinations by mingling many colors.

MASKING

A stamping technique in which an image or part of an image is covered to shield it from subsequent applications of color, masking is a great way to increase the versatility of your stamp collection. There are four basic ways to use a mask when stamping:

1. To create a background around a stamped image
2. To stamp an image so that it appears to be inside another stamped image (known as "mortise masking")
3. To isolate a portion of a stamp image
4. To create the illusion of depth by placing images behind and in front of one another

PREPARING A MASK

To prepare a mask for a rubber stamp, you'll need the following supplies:
- Dye-based stamp pad *or* marker
- Post-it™ notes *or* other removable adhesive notes
- Small scissors *or* a craft knife

1. Stamp the image on your project.
2. Prepare a mask of the image, position it over the stamp, then sponge color around it. If desired, make another mask to create a frame or defined shape of color. To keep from getting color on any surrounding surfaces, cover them with Post-it notes or scrap paper.
3. Remove the masks. If necessary, carefully fill in any gaps with a marker or the edge of a sponge. Reuse the masks to repeat the procedure, sponging on backgrounds in other colors.

1. Ink the stamp you're planning to mask with a dye-based ink or marker. (Dye-based inks are more suitable for preparing masks than pigment inks because their translucency makes it easier to align the mask over an image.)
2. Stamp the image on a Post-it note so that the sticky backing at the top of the note is on the back of the image.
3. Using scissors or a craft knife, cut out the image just within its outline so that it's slightly smaller than the stamped image. This will prevent a blank area or gap from appearing around the edges of the masked image.

CREATING A BACKGROUND

Masks are an excellent way to add colored backgrounds to stamped images. In this example, one Post-it note mask was used to cover the image while three others were used to create a square of color around it.

1   2   3

MORTISE MASKING

A *mortise* is a hole or slot into which part of something else fits. To prepare a mortise mask, a Post-it note is stamped with an image, then the image itself or a portion of it is cut out. This mask is placed over its stamped version so that when a second image is stamped over it, it will appear to fit inside it.

1. Stamp the image on your project. Re-ink and stamp the image on a Post-it note.
2. Carefully cut out the inner portion of the mask with a craft knife.
3. Place the mask over the original stamped image. Stamp a second image inside the cutout portion of the mask.

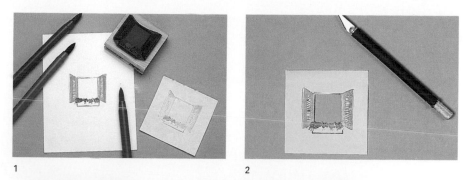

1   2

3

ISOLATING PART OF AN IMAGE

You can also use masks to isolate or abstract part of a stamped image. This technique is particularly effective in creating repetitive patterns. In this example, a sheet of white paper was trimmed at both ends to create a mask for a piece of green paper so that only part of the ginkgo leaf stamp would be printed.

1. Trim a sheet of paper so that only the area of the project to be stamped is exposed. This will also isolate a portion of the stamp; in this example, only the broad part of the ginkgo leaf was printed.
2. You can take this technique one step further by covering the first printing of images with Post-it note masks, then returning the large paper mask to its original position. Stamp a second row of images to achieve an "overlapping" repeat.

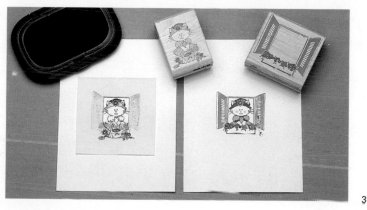

1   2

COMBINING IMAGES IN A SINGLE SCENE

Masking can also be used to make one image appear to be "behind" another. This effect is essential in creating the illusion of depth among a group of images or within a scene. In this example, ten stamps were combined to create a mountain vista featuring a galloping horse.

1. The foreground images—the two cacti, the horse, and the two parts of the fence—were stamped first, then masked.

2. The large tree, the walkway, and the cactus behind the fence were then stamped over the masks.

3. The masks of the foreground images were left in place, the second set of images were masked, and the mountains and a portion of the foreground cactus were stamped.

4. The clouds were stamped, then masked so that the sky could be sponged in blue.

5. The masks for the clouds and the tree were removed, then the pine needles were stamped.

6. With all of the masks in place, the grass was stamped, then sponged in green. Its color gradually decreases in intensity from foreground to background to suggest distance.

MASKING TIPS

- *Always cut more than one mask at a time.* Stamp the Post-it at the top of the stack, then remove several notes and cut them at the same time. Extra masks are particularly useful when you're sponging more than one background color and want to avoid transferring inks from a previously used mask.
- *Save your masks for future use.* Store them in the same boxes along with their stamps, or organize them in small envelopes.
- *Although many stampers make masks from lightweight or tracing papers,* these materials have a tendency to slip unless you use a tacky, removable adhesive to keep them in place.

CREATING DEPTH AND DIMENSION

In addition to masking, three other techniques can be used to create depth within stamped images: adding shadows, overprinting, and dimensional layering. These dimensional techniques are essentially confined to paper projects, such as greeting cards and pictures.

ADDING SHADOWS

Adding shadows to your stamped images is an easy way to imply form and create visual interest. The simplest method of adding shadows is to outline one side of a stamped image with a gray brush marker. In order to prevent visual chaos, you must be consistent about the position and quality of the light source that produces the shadows, particularly when you're adding them to several images within a scene or pattern.

OVERPRINTING

You can achieve interesting results by *overprinting* an image, or stamping one image over another in complementary or contrasting colors. Solid graphic images work best with this technique. Select two colors, then stamp the image in the lighter of the two colors. Clean the stamp, re-ink it with the darker color, then stamp it over the light print, but slightly off center. Experiment by stamping outline images over solid ones to create unusual patterns and textures.

The light source implied by the shadow on this stamp is below and to the left.

In this example of overprinting, yellow stars were overstamped with red ones to create an interesting pattern.

DIMENSIONAL IMAGES

Stamping is an excellent medium for creating dimensional images. By stamping, cutting out, and layering images with foam tape or dots, you can create depth within images and "elevate" your stamped art.

The card shown at left in the photograph below was begun with an embossed brick pattern, to which a wash of beige watercolor was added. The outer window frame, flower box, and flowers were stamped on another piece of card stock, and the window panes were stamped on acetate with permanent ink. Then all the images were cut out and layered with foam tape over the embossed brick pattern. The card at right utilized a pattern stamp to emboss a wide border, then a glue stick was used to add a thin embossed rule around the perimeter of the central space. The basket and sunflowers were stamped on separate pieces of card stock and carefully cut out. Before affixing the images to the patterned card with foam tape, the petals were curved by rubbing them against the bowl of a spoon. (This curving technique can also be seen in the Dimensional Partridge project, pages 140–141.)

The dinosaur diorama in the photograph at the bottom of the page consists of several layers of images that are held in place with an accordion frame. As in the other two examples, all the images in the diorama were stamped on separate pieces of card stock and layered with foam tape on top of the background, which was stamped first. After the front piece was stamped and die-cut, the accordion frame was created by folding strips of paper the same length as each side of the frame and affixing them to its edges, with the folds facing inward.

Shown at left and below are just a few examples of how stamps can be used to create dimensional images.

If your stamped compositions seem static and lack energy, you can try some of the following techniques to help create the effect of motion. Although motion is most evidently applicable to humorous projects such as greeting cards featuring cartoon characters, it can also be used with other motifs, such as falling leaves.

DRAGGING OR STREAKING

To simulate swift motion, stamp the image, then drag the stamp in the direction from which the image is approaching. If you prefer that the image itself remain unsmeared, lift the front portion of the stamp slightly, then drag it so that only the rear portion of the image leaves streaks. You could also mask the image, then create a dynamic "swoosh" with an inked foam sponge by sweeping a splash of color away from the image in the direction from which it is moving.

FADING OUT

This technique is effective for simulating slow or deliberate movement. Stamp the image and, without re-inking, stamp backwards two or three times, slightly overlapping the images. Tilt up the front portion of your stamp slightly so that only the rear fades out. For a more precise look, you can mask the main image, then back-stamp without re-inking.

Three examples of dragging or streaking: (Top) Masking the image to add a "whoosh" of color with a foam sponge; (near right) lifting the front of the stamp slightly and dragging only a portion of it so that the image remains unsmudged; (far right) dragging the entire stamp backward to simulate rapid motion.

Use the fade-out technique to simulate slow motion. Stamp the lead image, then stamp backward without re-inking, slightly overlapping the prints and tilting the stamp up so that only the back of the image is printed.

MASKING FOR MOTION

Masking is an effective way to simulate motion in an isolated area of an image. Simply select a central point within the image, cut a mask large enough to protect the stamping surface from a wide swath of several impressions, then use the fade-out technique.

ADDING HAND-DRAWN FLOURISHES

The designs of some stamps imply motion by incorporating simple lines, swirls, or squiggles. You can also add "action" lines of your own, and tailor them to suit the needs of a specific image or project. If you're feeling particularly creative, you can enhance the lines with the addition of color.

Some rubber stamp designs incorporate simple lines that indicate movement or gestures.

When combined with the fade-out technique, masking can also be used to produce motion in a specific area of an image.

Adding a hand-drawn flourish to a stamp allows you to tailor its motion to a project, and provides an opportunity to introduce your own unique brand of humor.

COMBINING IMAGES

Stamp images can also be used together to express motion. For instance, a cloud can be converted to a departing puff of exhaust by adding a few lines to it. For whimsical and fanciful images, stars, swirls, and bursts can signify movement. Word and letter stamps can also convey action—or inaction, as in the example below, right. Experiment by combining images that at first might appear to be incompatible or unrelated. You may be surprised at the results.

Simple lines and shapes can be enhanced with bold splashes of color.

Stamp images can often be combined to imply movement or action.

BACKGROUNDS

There are many ways to create a background that perfectly accents or embellishes your stamp art. A variety of background styles, including solid color, gradated color blends, textures, and patterns, are discussed and illustrated below. Keep in mind that the color and texture of a background always influence the color and presentation of the stamped images that it features, so be sure to test any combinations you're considering before committing to anything.

SPONGED BACKGROUNDS

Foam sponges are among the most versatile tools used with rubber stamps. In addition to coloring stamped images and inking rubber dies, foam wedge sponges provide an excellent means for coloring larger areas.

Pinch back the edges of the sponge so that its sharp edges won't leave an imprint on your project, then ink it by tamping it on a stamp pad or by rolling the tip of a brush marker against it. Since it's easier to work with a lightly loaded sponge, blot it on scrap paper before applying it to your project. Dab the color on the surface with a light blotting or brushing motion, reinking the sponge as needed. To maintain color consistency, sponge on color so it slightly overlaps any previously sponged areas. It may be necessary to sponge an area several times to achieve an even distribution of color. Use a separate wedge sponge for each color you apply to the project. Templates and masks can be sponged to create borders and edges. (See "Borders and Edges," pages 58–59.)

TEXTURED BACKGROUNDS

Sophisticated textured effects are within every stamper's reach. Unusual textures can be produced quickly and easily by crumpling paper towels, plastic wrap, tin foil, or waxed paper, inking them with single-color or rainbow stamp pads, and blotting them on the intended surface. Each "applicator" creates a different texture, ranging from soft, loosely spaced blotches to dense, well-defined patterns.

Also available are a variety of rubber stamps in such textures as marbles, plaids, sponging, and stippling, which can be used either individually or combined to create one-of-a-kind backgrounds.

The backgrounds in these two projects combine sponging and texturizing. First, crumpled plastic wrap (below, left) and paper (below, right) were inked in blue and blotted on the surface. Then green and red were sponged on, either in faint washes (left) or in defined blotches (right).

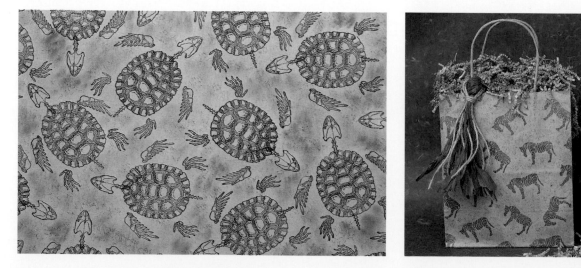

BRAYERED BACKGROUNDS

A rubber brayer provides a quick and easy way to create colorful backgrounds. To make a solid background, ink the entire surface of the brayer on a single-color stamp pad. (Dye-based and water-based inks appear more vivid, particularly on white coated papers, while pigment inks work best on uncoated papers, and provide a quick, easy way to make colored papers for collaging and layering projects.) Roll the inked brayer over the paper, overlapping each stroke until the desired shade is achieved. Streak marks gradually disappear as more color is applied. Use the same method with a rainbow stamp pad to produce a gradated background.

PLAIDS AND OTHER PATTERNS

The brayer's rubber roller can also be drawn on or stamped, then applied to a surface to create a continuous pattern or multiple images. To make a plaid, position the brayer so that the flat metal edge is lying flat on your work surface. Hold a brush marker in one hand so that the tip touches the rubber roller, then turn the roller with the other so that an unbroken line is drawn around its circumference. Repeat this procedure using brush markers in different colors and tip-widths, varying the space between the lines until the entire length of the roller has been inked with bands of color. Roll the brayer across the surface in one direction, then reorient the surface and crisscross the first set of lines with a second pass to produce the plaid. Although there's usually enough ink left on the roller to complete the second pass, if you prefer an intensely colored plaid you can re-ink the brayer in the same configuration of lines and colors before rolling it a second time. You can also use this technique to draw other patterns directly on the brayer, including random dots and patterned lines.

GHOSTING

To create "ghosted" backgrounds composed of subtle, shadowlike images, you'll need a rubber stamp; embossing ink, white, matte-finish coated card stock; a brayer; and a single-color dye-based ink stamp pad. Ink the stamp with embossing ink and stamp it on the card several times. (Do *not* apply embossing powder or heat.) Ink the brayer on the dye-based ink pad, then roll it over the card. Since the embossing ink acts as a resist, the images will begin to appear as more color is applied. These images can stand alone, or can be overprinted or embossed in a complementary or contrasting color for beautiful results.

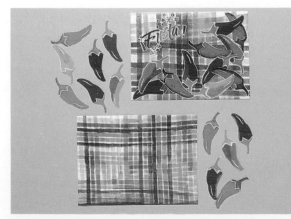

This colorful plaid serves as a background for a vivid assortment of stamped images, all of which were stamped on sticker paper, cut out, and affixed to the paper.

Here, snowflakes were embossed in white over "ghosted" flakes on a purple ground.

BORDERS AND EDGES

Borders and edges are made up of solid areas of color, texture, or patterns, both random and structured, that fall within a defined area. There are virtually no creative limitations on the decorative borders and edges you can make to complement your stamped images. By exploring and experimenting with different colors, patterns, and textures, you'll enrich all your stamp art projects.

RUBBER-STAMPED BORDERS

There are several ways to use stamps to create decorative borders or frames:

- *Stamp a single image several times in a row.* Use the long edge of a stamp positioning tool as a guide, or use a positioning tool with tracing paper to place images precisely.
- *Use one of the two types of stamps designed to yield borders:* a straight-border stamp, which is composed of several images; or a roller stamp.
- *Use a texture or pattern stamp with a mask to make a striking border.* Trim a large Post-it note so that it masks the central area of your project's surface. Stamp or emboss the image randomly over the exposed border, then remove the mask. For a more finished look, use a ruler and a fine-line marker to add a thin rule to the border's inside edge. For a colored background, cover the central area with a mask, sponge the exposed border with color, let dry, then stamp the pattern or texture in a contrasting or complementary color.
- *Use a few small images to create a loosely defined border.* If you use brush markers or dye-based inks, both of which are translucent, you can overprint the images in several different colors.

Simple borders can be stamped by repeating an individual image (left), or by using a predesigned straight-border (center) or roller stamp (right). Use the stamp positioning tool if necessary to align images precisely.

Masks can be used to design a wide range of borders. Masked borders can be stamped with a pattern (left), sponged with color and stamped (center) or embossed, and used to isolate a portion of an embossed or stamped image (right).

NARROW BORDERS AND EDGES

Straight, narrow borders and edges can be colored, embossed, or glittered. Regardless of medium, a cork-bottom metal ruler is essential for aligning a straight edge: Simply place the ruler far enough from the edge of the project to create the desired width. For a simple colored border or edge, run a wide brush marker against the ruler's edge to define the width of the area, then color it in. For an elegant embossed border or edge, apply a broad-tip glue pen or embossing pen against the edge of the ruler, fill in the entire area with glue or embossing ink, sprinkle with embossing powder, then melt the powder with an embossing heat tool. Clean the ruler with a damp paper towel to remove any adhesive before embossing the remaining edges. When making a glitter border, use a glue pen and omit the heat.

NOVELTY BORDERS AND EDGES

Novelty borders have three material requirements: a coloring medium such as ink or embossing powder; a piece of paper or card stock; and, most important, a pair of novelty-edge scissors. Create a template by cutting the four edges of the paper or card with the novelty-edge scissors so that it's smaller than your notecard or project. The size of the template will depend on how wide you want the border to be. To color the border, position the template on the surface of your project, ink the flat end of a wedge sponge on a stamp pad or with a brush marker, then apply the color within the border until the desired intensity is achieved. To emboss the border, ink a wedge sponge with embossing ink, apply the ink within the border, remove the template, sprinkle with embossing powder, then apply heat.

To make a novelty edge on a notecard, cut away a narrow portion of the front right-hand (for vertically oriented cards) or bottom edge (for horizontal formats) of the card with novelty-edge scissors so that the color on the inside edge of the card is revealed when the card is folded.

Ink a few stamp images with brush markers or dye-based inks and overprint them to make a less precise border.

Scallop-edge scissors were used to create the template for this novelty border.

The front right-hand edge of this card was trimmed with decorative-edge scissors to reveal a narrow sponged border on its inside edge.

PAPER PROJECTS

For most people, paper is the first surface that comes to mind when the words "rubber stamping" are mentioned. In fact, many a novice stamper's initial encounter with this craft involves paper, such as decorating envelopes to create correspondence art. Other beginner-level projects include greeting cards, invitations, stationery, and gift wrap, all of which are featured in this chapter. In most instances, the stamp images define, or at least guide, choices of paper, color, and even type of project.

AFRICAN WILDLIFE GIFT WRAP

Animal lovers of all ages will appreciate a gift wrapped in an exquisite paper trimmed with patterned paper "ribbons." Black raffia and jute string provide distinctive natural touches. This gift-wrap technique can be adapted to just about any stamp image, and will take on a completely different look when used with papers in contrasting or complementary colors and with other types of embellishments. Experiment with different ink colors, too.

MATERIALS
Project
Gift box
Stamps
Giraffe print (A853E)
Giraffe (A825E)
Inks
Black pigment ink stamp pad
Papers and Wrapping Supplies
Terracotta mulberry paper
Black mulberry paper
Black raffia
Jute string
Miscellaneous
Scissors
Metal ruler
Pencil
Glue stick
Post-it notes
Double-stick tape
Hole punch

VARIATIONS

To make the zebra gift wrap (see opposite), wrap a gift box with dark green mulberry paper and seal it with double-stick tape. Cut a piece of kraft paper large enough to wrap the width of the box. Ink a Zebra stamp (A826E) with black pigment ink and stamp it randomly on the kraft paper, let dry, then crumple it, flatten it out, and tear its edges so they're rough and irregular. Wrap the kraft paper around the gift box, then trim it with a torn "bow" of green paper twist.

GIRAFFE WRAPPING PAPER AND GIFT TAG

1. Cut a piece of terracotta mulberry paper large enough to wrap around your gift box. Make sharp creases in the paper at the edges of the front, back, and sides of the box. (See Photo 1.) Remove the paper from the box and set it aside.

2. Cut a strip of terracotta mulberry paper approximately 3 inches (7.6 cm) wide and long enough to wrap around the box. Use a ruler to measure and mark the edges of the strip lightly with a pencil, then sharply crease them to create folds. To achieve feathered, uneven edges along the lengths of the strip, hold the ruler down along the folds and tear the paper by pulling upwards.

3. Ink the giraffe print stamp with black ink and, working from top to bottom, stamp the strip so that the prints align point to point. Allow the ink to dry.

4. Tear a strip of black mulberry paper ½ inch (1.5 cm) wider than the stamped strip of terracotta paper. (See Photo 2.) Apply glue to the back of the terracotta strip and affix it to the center of the black strip. Set it aside.

5. Ink the giraffe stamp with black ink and stamp a few foreground giraffes on the terracotta wrapping paper. Use the crease marks as guides to positioning the giraffes on the bottom right-hand area of the front of the box. (See Photo 3.)

6. Use a Post-it note to make a mask for the giraffe stamp. Place it over a foreground giraffe before stamping an adjacent giraffe in the background. Repeat this step to stamp other background giraffes. Allow the ink to dry.

7. Wrap the box with the giraffe paper using double-stick tape. Wrap the giraffe print strip around the box, positioning it toward the left-hand side. (The joining seams should be on the back.) Wrap several strands of black raffia and jute around the top of the box and tie them so that the knot is in the front.

8. Tear the terracotta paper to make a rectangle measuring 2½ × 3 inches (6.5 × 7.6 cm). Stamp a giraffe in the center of the paper with black ink.

9. Tear the black paper to make a rectangle ½ inch (1.3 cm) larger than the terracotta tag, and glue it to the back. Punch a hole in the top left-hand corner of the tag, thread it with jute, and tie it to the raffia and jute ribbon.

1

2

3

63

STAINED GLASS GRAPE CARD

Stamp images that feature large, blank areas are an open invitation for stampers to experiment with different color media. For example, you can use opaque color to create a bold, flat look, or translucent or semi-transparent media like brush markers, colored pencils, or watercolors for a blended effect. For some ideas on how to more fully exploit the "stained glass" aspect of the image featured in this project, refer to the Variations box on the opposite page.

MATERIALS

Stamps
Grape (A1241G)

Inks and Embossing Powders
Black pigment ink stamp pad
Clear embossing powder

Brush Markers
Violet
Pale green
Medium reddish brown

Papers
8½- × 11-inch
(21.6- × 28-cm) sheet of white parchment paper

Miscellaneous
Embossing heat tool

VARIATIONS

Here are a few suggestions on how to "put a gloss on" this stained glass grape, or create luster in other images that suggest reflection:

- *To enhance the colors' transparency*, stamp on a translucent vellum paper.

- *Create colored "panes"* by cutting away the open areas of the image and either pasting color papers behind them or coloring the interior of the card.

- *To create a shiny raised surface*, color the image with brush markers with an even application of color. Using a glue stick, apply glue to the entire image. Sprinkle with clear embossing powder, remove the excess, and heat to melt.

- *Achieve a textural look* by applying puff paint to the open areas of the image.

1. Create the card by folding a vertically oriented sheet of parchment paper in half from top to bottom.
2. Ink the grape stamp with black pigment ink and stamp it on the left-hand side of the front of the card. Sprinkle the image with clear embossing powder, tap off the excess, then melt it with the embossing heat tool.
3. Using violet for the grapes, pale green for the leaves, and reddish brown for the branches, color the image with the brush markers. (See photo below.) Create highlights and shading by applying more ink around the outlines of each element.
4. Handwrite your message on the right-hand side of the card.

65

HYDRANGEA GIFT WRAP

The radiant beauty of hydrangeas is portrayed in this gift-wrap project by blending stamp inks directly on the rubber die—two colors each for the flowers and the foliage. For successful color blending, remember to ink each element of the stamp with the lightest color first, then add progressively darker hues. Use the lighter of two colors to create a gradual shift between them.

MATERIALS

Project
Gift box

Stamps
Hydrangea (Z521E)

Inks
Hot pink pigment ink stamp pad
Lavender pigment ink stamp pad
Emerald green pigment ink stamp pad
Pine green pigment ink stamp pad

Papers and Wrapping Supplies
Light pink mulberry paper
Variegated pink French wire ribbon
Hydrangea sprig (optional)

Miscellaneous
Double-stick tape
Scissors

VARIATIONS

To make an original gift, use this decorated mulberry wrap to cover a box, journal, or picture frame, or to make a coordinated desk set.

1. Cut a piece of pink mulberry paper so that it's large enough to wrap around your gift box, with overlap to allow for the width of the double-stick tape.

2. Apply the hot pink and lavender inks directly to the blossom portion of the rubber die. Apply the hot pink (the lighter of the two colors) first, then use the lavender as an accent. (See photo below.) Using the emerald and pine green inks, repeat this procedure for the hydrangea's leaves.

3. Stamp the mulberry paper in a random pattern, re-inking the stamp after each impression.

4. Allow the prints to dry thoroughly before wrapping your box. Seal it with double-stick tape and decorate it with French wire ribbon. If desired, insert a sprig of hydrangea into the knot of the bow.

MIXED-PATTERN NOTECARD

Pattern stamps provide a creative way to design a wide assortment of cards. By using one color scheme for several images, it's possible to combine what might at first appear to be unrelated or conflicting images.

MATERIALS

Stamps
Plaid weave (A910E)
Scattered roses (A915E)
Rose mosaic (A850E)

Inks and Embossing Powders
Wild iris pigment ink stamp pad
Clear embossing powder
Black pigment ink stamp pad
Embossing ink stamp pad

Brush Markers
Violet
Leaf green
Magenta

Papers
Desert sand folded notecard and postcard
Purple paper (to match the violet brush marker)
Green paper (optional)

Miscellaneous
Embossing heat tool
Stamp positioning tool (optional)
Post-it notes
Scissors
Low-temperature glue gun
Novelty ribbon trim

1. Ink the plaid stamp on the wild iris pigment ink pad and stamp it on the folded notecard approximately 1 inch (2.5 cm) from its top and left-hand edges. (See Photo 1.) Sprinkle the print with clear embossing powder, tap off the excess, and melt it with the embossing heat tool.

2. Continue to stamp and emboss the plaid image in a rectangle shape until the pattern bleeds off the right-hand and bottom edges of the notecard. You can either approximate the placement of each print or use a stamp positioning tool for more accurate placement.

3. Ink over alternate vertical lines and the perimeter of the plaid pattern with the violet brush marker, and alternate horizontal lines with the leaf green marker. (See Photo 2.)

4. Mask the plaid pattern with Post-it notes. Ink the scattered roses stamp with black pigment ink and stamp it in the remaining space on the left-hand side and along the top of the notecard. (See Photo 3.) Sprinkle each print with embossing powder, remove the excess, and melt it with the embossing tool. Use the leaf green and magenta brush markers to color the embossed roses.

5. Ink the rose mosaic stamp with embossing ink. While the die is still wet, ink the rose portion of the die with the magenta brush marker, the leaves with the leaf green marker, and the border with the violet marker. (See Photo 4.) Stamp the rose mosaic on the postcard and emboss it with the clear powder. Cut out the image, leaving a slight margin of space around it.

6. Cut a square of purple paper so that it measures about 1/4 inch (0.64 cm) larger on all sides than the border of the rose mosaic stamp. Using the glue gun, glue the rose mosaic cutout to the purple square, then glue the mounted cutout to the lower right-hand side of the notecard. Glue the novelty ribbon to the top left-hand corner of the plaid pattern.

7. If desired, mount the notecard on a rectangle of purple paper about 1/4 inch (0.64 cm) larger on all sides than the notecard, then on green paper about 1/4 inch (0.64 cm) larger than the purple paper.

1

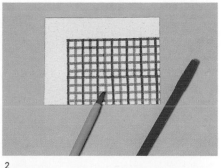

2

3

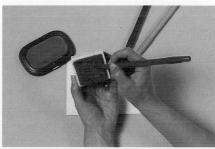

4

RED ROSE STATIONERY SET

It's easy to make your own romantic stationery with rubber stamps and colored pencils. This four-piece set includes bordered letter paper, a "Thinking of You" notecard, an unusual greeting card with a folded flap featuring a garland of roses, and a coordinating envelope. Anyone who receives one of your handcrafted notes will appreciate your thoughtfulness and admire your creativity.

MATERIALS

Stamps
For the stationery
Romantic rose (A805B)
For the envelope
Romantic rose with stem (A806E)

Inks
Black pigment ink stamp pad

Papers
Cream parchment stationery paper and envelope

Pens and Pencils
Pink and green colored pencils
Gold metallic fine-point pen

Miscellaneous
Scissors
Scrap paper
Metal ruler

ROSE BORDER STATIONERY

1. Create a rectangular mask by cutting a piece of scrap paper so that it measures approximately 1 inch (2.54 cm) smaller on all sides than a sheet of the stationery. Place the mask over one of the sheets, leaving a uniform border exposed on all four sides.
2. Ink the rose stamp and stamp it randomly around the border while holding the mask in place. (See Photo 1.) Remove the mask and allow the ink to dry.
3. Color the images with the colored pencils. (See Photo 2.)
4. Aligning the ruler against each edge of the border, use the gold metallic pen to draw thin gold rules around the perimeter of the writing area and on the edges of the stationery. (See Photo 3.)

ROSE-TRIMMED ENVELOPE

1. Ink the rose stem stamp with black pigment ink, then stamp it on the center of the envelope's flap. Allow the ink to dry.
2. Color the image with the colored pencils.
3. Use the ruler and the gold metallic pen to draw a thin gold rule around the edge of the flap. (See Photo 4.)

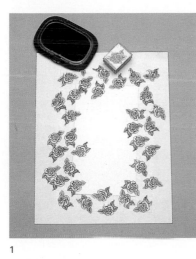

1

2

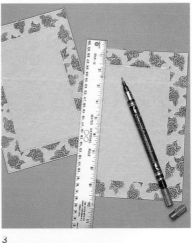

3

4

MATERIALS

Stamps

"Thinking of You" (A861E)

Romantic rose with stem (A806E)

Inks and Embossing Powders

Embossing stamp pad

Gold embossing powder

Black pigment ink stamp pad

Papers

Cream parchment folded notecard

Cream parchment postcard

Miscellaneous

Embossing heat tool

Ruler

Glue pen

Pink and green colored pencils

Victorian-edge scissors (M9210)

"THINKING OF YOU" NOTECARD

1. Use the embossing ink, gold embossing powder, and embossing heat tool to stamp and emboss "Thinking of You" on the front of the folded notecard. Position the sentiment on the right-hand side of the card. (See Photo 1.)

2. Cut a 2½-inch-wide × 3½-inch-long (6.4 × 9 cm) rectangle from the postcard. Use the ruler and glue pen to create a border of glue approximately ⅔ inch (1.7 cm) wide. Sprinkle the glue with embossing powder, then melt the powder with the embossing tool.

3. Use the ruler and glue pen to create a border of glue ½ inch (1.3 cm) wide on the inside bottom edge of the folded notecard. Sprinkle the glue with embossing powder, then use the embossing tool to melt the powder. (See Photo 2.)

4. Cut another rectangle measuring 2 × 3 inches (5 × 7.6 cm) from the leftover postcard. Ink the rose stamp with black ink and stamp it in the center of the card. Let dry, then color with the colored pencils. (See Photo 3.)

5. Trim the front bottom edge of the folded notecard and all four sides of the gold-bordered postcard with the Victorian-edge scissors.

6. Use the glue pen to adhere the rose-stamped card to the gold-bordered card. Glue to left side of folded notecard. (See Photo 4.)

1

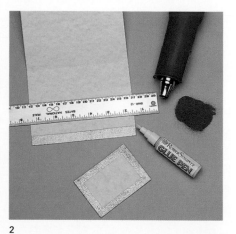

2

3

4

MATERIALS
Stamps
Romantic rose garland
(A800F)
Romantic rose (A805B)
Inks
Black dye-based ink
stamp pad
Black pigment ink stamp
pad
Papers
Tracing paper
Cream parchment folded
notecard
Pens, Pencils, and
Markers
Colored pencils in
assorted colors
Pink fine-point marker
Gold metallic pen
Miscellaneous
Scallop-edge scissors
(M9201)
Stamp positioning tool
Cutting mat
Craft knife
Narrow (1/4-inch
[0.64-cm]) gold ribbon

ROSE GARLAND CARD

1. Fold a large piece of tracing paper in half and insert it into the notecard so that the folds align. Trim the edges of the card and tracing paper with the scallop-edge scissors. (See Photo 1.) Set the trimmed tissue paper aside.

2. Use the stamp positioning tool, another piece of tracing paper, and the black dye-based ink to create a template of the rose garland stamp.

3. Open the notecard and position the rose garland stamp template to position the image at a slight angle in the upper left-hand portion of the left-hand side of the card. (Avoid positioning it near the center.) Align the corner of the stamp positioning tool with the corner of the template, remove the template, then ink the rose garland stamp with black pigment ink and stamp it. (See Photo 2.) Let dry before coloring with colored pencils.

4. Lay the card open on the cutting mat. Use the craft knife to cut along the right edge of the rose garland, then close the card. (See Photo 3.)

5. Ink the romantic rose stamp with black pigment ink. Working only within the area to the left of the cut that silhouettes the bottom of the rose garland image, stamp the front of the notecard randomly with several roses. Allow the ink to dry before coloring them with colored pencils.

6. Gently fold back the upper right corner of the front of the card so that the rose garland lies flat, then crease the fold. (See Photo 4.)

7. Use the pink marker to add trios of tiny dots to the area of the folded flap to the left of the garland. Carefully outline the scalloped edges of the notecard, both inside and out, with the gold metallic pen.

8. Assemble the card by inserting the scallop-trimmed tracing paper into the notecard and tying it into place with the gold ribbon. (See Photo 5.)

1

2

5

3

4

STAMPED WATERCOLOR ART CARDS

By combining soft washes of watercolor with rubber stamp images, a simple composition can be embellished quickly and easily. The cards shown below represent only a few of the potential approaches to this unusual form of mixed media. (The supplies listed on the opposite page were used to create the kimono card; the others incorporate stamps from other sets.) Stamp your images only after the underlying washes have dried completely, and be sure to avoid touching the stamp inks with the wet brush when adding final details.

Stamps
Petite basic shapes
(740.01)
Japanese art collection
(760.02)
Inks
Pine green pigment ink
stamp pad
Chestnut brown pigment
ink stamp pad
Cornflower blue pigment
ink stamp pad
Dusty rose pigment ink
stamp pad
Watercolor Supplies
Watercolor paper
Watercolor paints (in
various colors)
Watercolor brushes
Miscellaneous
Kraft tape
Medium-soft pencil
Kneaded eraser

1. Before you begin, you must stretch the watercolor paper to keep it from buckling and wrinkling when you paint on it. Immerse the paper in cold or room-temperature water for several minutes. (Avoid creasing the paper, as it will tend to split at the creases as it stretches.) Transfer the saturated sheet to your work surface. To flatten the paper and squeeze excess water from it, use the side of your hand to carefully press the sheet from its center toward its edges, blotting the excess water from the edges as you work. Moisten the kraft tape and use it to affix the sheet to a smooth, flat surface. Allow the paper to dry.

2. With the pencil, loosely sketch the composition in simple shapes. Once the sketch is complete, lighten the pencil lines by shaping the kneaded eraser into a ball and rolling it over the paper with the palm of your hand.

3. Begin painting by applying light washes of color to each shape. Let each wash dry before applying the second and third washes, to add shading, highlights, and accents of color.

4. Once the watercolors have dried, you can begin stamping. In the card shown below, stamped bamboo leaves provide foliage for a painted plant, swirls decorate its pot, a sprinkling of flowers creates a pattern for the kimono, and a square motif was used to design a tiled surface.

5. After stamping all the images, use a small watercolor brush to add final details to your painting. Do not stroke the stamped elements with the moistened brush or they will smear.

PAPER JEWELRY

Making paper jewelry with rubber stamps is remarkably easy. The stamp-and-glaze technique demonstrated here, which is illustrated on an Amish-style quilting square, can be adapted to virtually any image and color scheme. Text-weight paper doesn't have enough body, so be sure to use card stock. The textile markers won't run or bleed when brushed with the water-based glaze, which stiffens the paper and adds a wonderful glossy sheen.

MATERIALS
Stamps
Tulip quilt (A901C)
Inks and Embossing Powders
Clear embossing ink stamp pad
Gold embossing powder
Textile or Permanent Markers
Pink
Green
Paper
Desert sand postcard
Miscellaneous
Scissors
Glue stick
⅛-inch (0.32-cm) hole punch
Water-based transparent glaze
Flat acrylic paint brush
Jewelry needlenose pliers
Jewelry findings (French hooks for pierced earrings)

VARIATIONS
To make a matching pin, stamp and emboss an additional square, color it with textile markers, then apply five coats of transparent glaze to each side. Glue a pin finding to the back of the square to complete. A bunch of pins, each in a different block pattern, would make great gifts for your quilting friends.

TULIP QUILT BLOCK EARRINGS

1. With the embossing ink and the gold embossing powder, stamp and emboss four tulip squares on the postcard.
2. Cut out the squares, leaving a narrow margin of space around each one.
3. Use the pink textile marker to color the flowers and the border, and the green textile marker to color the stems and leaves. (See Photo 1.)
4. Glue two squares wrong sides together with the glue stick. Repeat with the two other squares. Cover the glued squares with a heavy book or another flat, heavy object until they are firmly fused together. Allow to set overnight.
5. Apply glaze to one side of each square; let dry. Turn the squares over and apply glaze to the other side; let dry. Punch a hole in the top corner of each square. Apply four more coats of glaze to each side of the two squares. (See Photo 2.)
6. Use the needlenose pliers to attach the earring findings to the glazed squares.

1

2

HOME DECOR

If nothing else, the range of surfaces used for projects in this section proves the versatility of rubber stamping beyond the shadow of a doubt. These projects, which include a frame painted and embossed with the deep hues of autumn, a plain pine box embellished with butterflies and finished with a glossy acrylic glaze, and melamine plates stamped with playful vegetable designs, all make rubber stamping a sophisticated element of home decor. As is the case for all the projects in this book, you can choose to follow the material lists and instructions to the letter, or use the featured colors and stamp images solely as inspiration for your own original designs.

EMBOSSED ANIMAL SKIN PRINT MATS

These dramatic, easy-to-make mats require only a simple wood frame as a finishing touch. The instructions for embossing and using the stamp positioning tool apply to both the tiger and jaguar prints. The dimensions of the mat used to demonstrate the technique are 8 × 10 inches (20.3 × 25.4 cm) with a 5- × 7-inch (12.7- × 17.8-cm) window. Clear embossing ink and metallic embossing powders were used to create both designs shown below, but you can use pigment ink with clear embossing powder to match the color scheme of a room.

MATERIALS

Project
Photo or picture mats
Stamps
For the tiger print mat
Tiger print (A855E)
For the jaguar print mat
Jaguar stamp (A854E)
Inks and Embossing Powders
Black dye-based ink stamp pad
Clear embossing ink stamp pad
For the tiger print mat
Gold embossing powder
For the jaguar print mat
Copper embossing powder
Miscellaneous
Stamp positioning tool
Tracing paper
Embossing heat tool
Glue pen

VARIATIONS

- Animal skin patterns "change their spots" completely when stamped or embossed in unusual colors. Devise a color scheme for your mat so that it coordinates with a specific room decor.
- Stamp or emboss a mat using the giraffe-print stamp featured in the gift wrap project on pages 62–63.
- Stamp the patterns randomly, or use the stamp positioning tool to create a zigzag design.

1. Use the black dye-based ink and the stamp positioning tool to create a tracing-paper template for the pattern stamp.
2. Position the tracing-paper template over the top left-hand corner of the mat. Align the corner of the stamp positioning tool with the corner of the template, ink the pattern stamp with embossing ink, remove the template, and stamp the pattern, aligning the corner of its block with the corner of the positioning tool. Sprinkle the print with embossing powder in the color of your choice, tap to remove excess, and melt with the embossing heat tool.
3. Place the tracing-paper template to the right of the embossed image, positioning it so that the two appear seamless. Align the corner of the stamp positioning tool with the corner of the template, remove the template, stamp the pattern with embossing ink, and emboss. Repeat the process until the top border of the mat has been completed.
4. Repeat step 3 to complete the left-hand border first. Next stamp the bottom border, then the right-hand border, to the points indicated in Photo 1.
5. Align the tracing-paper template with each of the last prints on the right-hand and bottom borders so that the area on the top right-hand side of the pattern merges with the bottom left-hand edge of the last print on the right-hand border, and the area on the lower left of the pattern merges with the upper right-hand edge of the last print on the bottom border. (See Photo 2.) Use the stamp positioning tool to stamp the pattern with embossing ink, then emboss.
6. Complete the mat by stamping and embossing the remaining areas in the following sequence: (1) the edge of the right-hand border immediately to the right of the corner print; (2) the area of the bottom border immediately below the corner print; and (3) the lower right-hand corner of the mat. Isolate the corresponding area of the pattern so that the overall design is consistent.
7. Eliminate any conspicuous areas of demarcation between the patterns by touching them up with a glue pen and embossing powder.
8. If desired, embellish a second mat by using a glue pen to adhere embossing powder to its inner edge. (See Photo 3.)

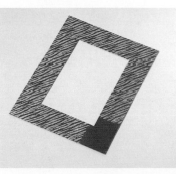

1

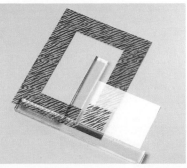

2

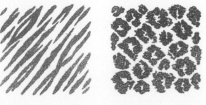

3

AUTUMN LEAVES FRAME

The layered design of this frame fully exploits a rich palette of fall colors. A harvest gold ground is stenciled with blocks of rust and dark green, lightly glazed with gold, then embossed with a random pattern of leaves. The unfinished wood frame used in this project measures $11 \times 12\frac{1}{2}$ inches (28×32 cm) and has a 5- × 7-inch (12.7- × 17.8-cm) window, making its borders broad enough to accommodate the bold design. Unfinished frames can be purchased at art supply and crafts stores, or you can make one yourself.

MATERIALS

Project
Unfinished wood frame

Stamps
Maple leaf (272D)
Oak leaf (268D)

Inks
Pine green pigment ink
stamp pad
Clear embossing ink
stamp pad

Embossing Powders
Clear embossing powder
Gold embossing powder
Copper embossing
powder

Acrylic Paints
Harvest gold
Rust
Dark green
Gold metallic

Miscellaneous
Sandpaper
Tack cloth
Acrylic paint brushes
Low-adhesive paper tape
Ruler
Wedge-shaped foam
sponge *or* stencil brush
(for painting the square
masks)
Wedge-shaped foam
sponge (for applying the
gold metallic paint)
Scrap paper
Embossing heat tool

VARIATIONS
Paint, glaze, and emboss
your frame in a color
scheme that coordinates
with a specific room, or
reflects another seasonal
theme.

1. Lightly sand the rough edges and surface of the frame until smooth. Wipe thoroughly with a tack cloth to remove sanding dust.
2. Paint the entire frame with one coat of harvest gold acrylic. Let dry.
3. Using the paper tape and a ruler, mask off rectangles in various sizes, leaving areas of harvest gold in between. (The shapes don't have to be perfect.) Use a foam sponge or stencil brush to paint the rectangles with rust and dark green acrylic. (See Photo 1.) Carefully remove the tape, then allow the paint to dry.
4. Dip a foam sponge into the gold metallic paint. Blot off the excess and apply a very thin coat in the direction of the surface grain. (See Photo 2.) Let dry.
5. On a piece of scrap paper, emboss several prints of both leaves using the pine green pigment ink with the clear embossing powder and the gold and copper embossing powders. Cut them out.
6. Position the scrap paper prints on the frame in a random design. (See Photo 3.) Removing one leaf at a time, stamp and emboss each with the appropriate ink and embossing powder. (Note that it's more efficient to stamp and emboss one color at a time.)

1

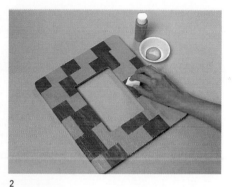

2

3

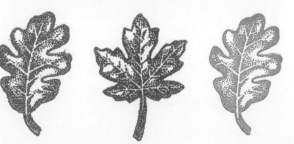

BUTTERFLY BOX

Use rubber stamps and colored pencils to transform a humble unfinished pine box into an attractive storage place for your jewelry, some matching stationery, or even a butterfly collection. The box is lightly sealed before stamping with a clear acrylic spray to prevent the ink from bleeding into the wood. Although neither the pigment ink nor the colored pencils require a protective finish, the glossy acrylic glaze intensifies the colors of both and warms the tone of the pine.

MATERIALS

Project
Unfinished hinged wood box

Stamps
Victorian butterfly stamp kit (951.57)

Inks
Black pigment ink stamp pad

Miscellaneous
Sandpaper
Tack cloth
Matte-finish acrylic spray sealer
Low-adhesive paper tape
Colored pencils (in assorted colors)
½-inch (1.3 cm) flat paint brush
Gloss-finish water-based acrylic glaze

VARIATIONS
If you're making this box as a gift, consider whether the recipient would also enjoy writing their personal correspondence on matching notecards (see opposite).

1. Sand the box to a smooth finish. Wipe it thoroughly with a tack cloth to remove sanding dust.
2. Lightly spray the box with the acrylic spray sealer. Let dry.
3. To keep the lid in place during stamping, tape it closed with a small piece of low-adhesive paper tape. Using black pigment ink, stamp three large butterflies on the front, five assorted butterflies on the top, and one large butterfly on each side of the box. (See Photo 1.) Let the prints dry for at least 24 hours.
4. Color the stamp images with the colored pencils. (See Photo 2.) If desired, use the colored pencils to draw freehand foliage or flowers to accent the butterfly prints.
5. Apply a coat of gloss-finish acrylic glaze to the entire box, taking care to keep the lid from sticking closed. (See Photo 3.) Let dry thoroughly before applying a second coat.

1

2

3

MELAMINE VEGETABLE PLATES

With a Make A Plate™ kit, you can use rubber stamps to design a plate to commemorate a birthday or anniversary, celebrate a holiday, or complement your kitchen decor. Simply stamp your design on the plate form included in the kit and send it to the manufacturer, who reproduces it on a melamine plate. You'll receive the finished plate in six to eight weeks. Make A Plate kits can be purchased in better toy stores.

The plate designs in this project were created by blending color with brush markers, masking, and sponging. Imagine using a set of these brightly colored plates on a picnic or to dine alfresco on a warm summer evening.

MATERIALS

Project
Melamine plate (from the Make A Plate kit)

Stamps
Terrific beet (Z583C)
Crunchy carrot (Z585E)

Brush Markers
Cherry
Green
Light green
Ochre
Orange

Miscellaneous
Scissors
Scrap paper
Pencil (with a round eraser)
Craft knife
Post-it notes
Two wedge-shaped foam sponges

VARIATIONS

- *For the beet plate (see opposite),* use the Terrific beet stamp (Z583C) with cherry, green, light green, and ochre brush markers.
- *For the shallot plate (see opposite),* use the Chef's shallot stamp (Z584C) with the green, light green, ochre, and magenta brush markers.

BEET AND CARROT PLATE

1. Cut a scrap-paper template of the round paper form from the plate kit. Use a pencil to draw a smaller circle in the center of the template approximately 5 inches (12.7 cm) in diameter. Carefully cut out the center circle with the craft knife and set it aside. (See Photo 1.)

2. Place the large template over the round paper form from the kit. Ink the beet portion of the beet stamp with the cherry marker, and ink the leaves by blending the green and light green markers directly on the stamp. Randomly stamp the beets within the cutout of the template, re-inking the stamp after making each print. (See Photo 2.)

3. Make three beet masks with Post-it notes, then use them to cover three adjacent beets. Ink the flat edge of a wedge sponge with the ochre brush marker, blotting any excess on a piece of scrap paper. Sponge the ochre ink over the beet masks to cover the white background. (See Photo 3.) Reposition the masks to complete the sponging of the entire center circle. Let dry.

4. Remove the large template and cover the stamped portion of the plate form with the small one. Ink the carrot stamp with the orange and green markers. Randomly stamp the carrots around the border, re-inking the stamp after making each print.

5. Make three carrot masks with Post-it notes. (Since the background border will be sponged in green, it's only necessary to make masks for the carrot portion of the stamp.) Working on a section at a time, place the three carrot masks over the stamped carrots. Ink the flat edge of a wedge sponge with the light green marker, blotting any excess on scrap paper. Keeping the small template in place and repositioning the carrot masks as necessary, sponge color around the border of the plate until it's complete. (See Photo 4.)

6. Ink the pencil eraser with the cherry marker. Stamp dots randomly among the carrots.

7. Follow the kit instructions to complete the plate.

1

2

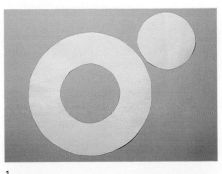

3

4

DECORATIVE TERRACOTTA TILES

Terracotta tiles can be stamped or embossed to coordinate with any decor. In this project, vibrant blue and green pigment inks were embossed with clear embossing powder to create lustrous raised images. Experiment with different pattern stamps to create your own unique designs. Before choosing a site to display your creativity, keep in mind that these tiles are for decorative purposes only and should not be installed in areas that are subject to moisture or heavy foot traffic, or on surfaces that require vigorous scrubbing.

MATERIALS
Project
Terracotta tiles
Stamps
Mosaic rubber stamp kit
(951.04)
Inks and Embossing Powders
Royal blue pigment ink stamp pad
Pine green pigment ink stamp pad
Clear embossing powder
Miscellaneous
Acrylic spray sealer
Small paint brush
Embossing heat tool

1. Seal the terracotta tiles very lightly with a coat of acrylic spray sealer. Let dry.
2. Stamp one element of the pattern with pigment ink, then sprinkle with embossing powder. Tap off the excess, then use the paint brush to remove any stray particles of powder. Melt the powder with the embossing heat tool. (See photo below.) Note that embossing powder takes longer to melt on terracotta than it does on paper.
3. Continue to stamp and emboss until the pattern is complete.

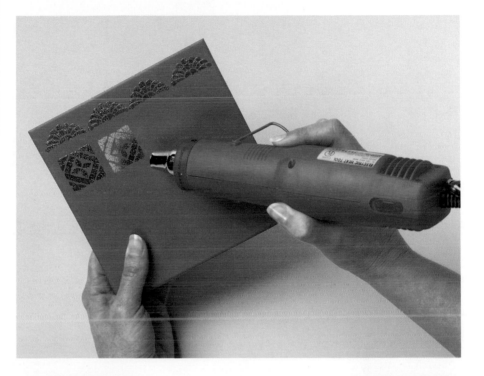

GIFT IDEAS

The best kind of gift—both to give *and* to receive—is one that's handmade. These gifts reflect the personalities of both the giver and the recipient, conveying the creativity, imagination, and affection of the former while fulfilling preferences for color, design, and interest of the latter. The projects in this chapter, which range from simple Japanese-style paper gift boxes to wearable stamped art, lie well within the grasp of even a beginning stamper, and can be easily adapted to suit any style or taste.

JAPANESE PAPER GIFT BOXES

Although paper was invented in China, the Japanese eventually became the most accomplished papermakers and -crafters in the world. Adorning the gift boxes featured in this project are adaptations of ancient Japanese *mon,* geometric and abstract designs based on natural forms that were used as family crests. Originally employed as stencil designs for dyed fabrics, *mon* played an important role in the development of *kiri-e,* or "cut-art," a traditional Japanese art form in which these designs are cut from paper and either painted or layered with colored papers.

Use these simple, elegant boxes to present small yet precious gifts. When you come across an unusual or interesting box or package design, add its pattern to your collection by unfolding it and tracing its outline.

MATERIALS

Patterns
For the petal box
Page 148
For the pyramid box
Page 149

Stamps
Selected designs from the Japanese art collection (760.02)

Inks and Embossing Powders
For the petal box
Embossing ink stamp pad
Gold embossing powder
For the pyramid box
Violet pigment ink stamp pad

Papers
Two 9-inch (22.9-cm) squares of card stock (one for each box) in colors of your choice

Miscellaneous
Pencil
Scissors *or* craft knife and cutting mat
Metal ruler
Bone folder
For the petal box
Embossing heat tool
Gold metallic pen
For the pyramid box
⅛-inch (0.32-cm) hole punch
Gold metallic paste
Paper towel (optional)
Thin gold cord

VARIATIONS

Use spray adhesive to glue handmade or art papers wrong side down to the right side of the card stock before cutting them both to the pattern. See the Fern Stationery and Gift Box project, pages 94–95, for an example of this technique.

CUTTING AND SCORING

- Using one of the methods outlined on pages 146–147, enlarge the pattern to full size. Transfer the pattern, including the score lines, to a piece of card stock. Mark the score lines lightly with a pencil.
- Following the pattern lines, cut the card stock to the dimensions of the box. Do not cut the score lines.
- To score the folds, align the ruler with each score line, then lightly run the pointed edge of the bone folder along the ruler's edge. Erase the pencil lines.

PETAL BOX

1. Working so that each flap overlaps the one immediately next to it, fold the flaps back onto the base of the box, tucking them down securely.
2. Ink the selected image with embossing ink, then stamp it in the center of the exposed area of one of the flaps. Sprinkle it with gold embossing powder, tap off the excess, and melt the powder with the embossing heat tool. Stamp and emboss the remaining four flaps. (See Photo 1.)
3. Unfold the flaps. Outline the edge of each flap with the gold metallic pen. Let dry, then place the gift inside the box before folding it closed as described above in step 1.

PYRAMID BOX

1. As indicated on the pattern, punch a hole at the top of each triangular area of the box.
2. To create the subtle gold sheen shown on the pyramid box on the opposite page, apply gold metallic paste to the four triangular areas and the square base of the box. To apply the paste, stroke it with your index finger, then rub your finger over the surface of the box to distribute the color evenly. (See Photo 2.) If desired, use a paper towel to apply the paste.
3. Ink the selected stamp with violet ink. Working from base to point in each triangular area of the box, stamp the image in a 3-2-1 configuration. Let dry.
4. Assemble the box by folding along the score lines. Close the box by lacing gold cord through the holes at the top of each side of the pyramid.

1

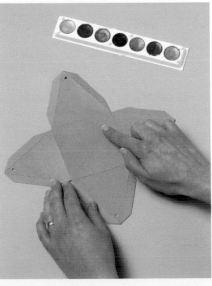

2

FERN STATIONERY AND GIFT BOX

This boxed stationery set—a celebration of green—is just right for nature lovers. The notecards, envelopes, and coordinating envelope-style gift box are all easy to make. All the elements of this project feature color blending, in which a comparatively light color, then successively darker ones, are applied to create exquisite shading. The stamps on the gift box are also embossed with clear embossing powder, for a lustrous, protective finish.

MATERIALS

Pattern
Page 150

Stamps
Monkey fern (A1102E)

Inks and Embossing Powders
Emerald green pigment ink stamp pad
Pine green pigment ink stamp pad
Clear embossing powder

Papers
For the stationery
Ten 4³/₄- × 6¹/₂-inch (12- × 16.5-cm) desert sand notecards and envelopes
For the box
One 11- × 17-inch (27.9- × 43.2-cm) piece of ochre mulberry paper
One 11- × 17-inch (27.9- × 43.2-cm) piece of lightweight cardboard

Miscellaneous
Scissors
Embossing heat tool
Pencil
Craft knife
Metal ruler
Cutting mat
Spray adhesive
Blank newsprint
Bone folder
White glue
Jute string

STATIONERY

1. Apply the emerald and pine green inks to the stamp by dabbing the pads directly on the die. First apply the emerald green (the lighter of the two colors) to the top of the foliage, then use the pine green to accent the lower part.
2. Stamp the cover of the notecard in a random, dense pattern, re-inking the stamp after making each print. Stamp a single horizontal fern on the flap of the envelope.
3. Repeat steps 1 and 2 for the remaining notecards and envelopes.

GIFT BOX

1. Cut the mulberry paper to 15¹/₂ × 10¹/₂ inches (39.4 × 26.7 cm).
2. Dab the emerald green stamp pad directly on the die, inking only the upper part of the foliage, then ink the lower part with the pine green stamp pad.
3. Stamp the image on the mulberry paper, then emboss it with clear embossing powder. Continue stamping and embossing the paper to achieve a random, widely spaced pattern. Set it aside.
4. Using one of the methods outlined on pages 146–147, enlarge the pattern for the gift box to full size. Transfer the pattern, including the score lines, to the cardboard. Lightly mark the score lines in pencil.
5. Following the pattern lines, use the craft knife, ruler, and cutting mat to cut the cardboard to the dimensions of the box. Do not cut the score lines.
6. Lightly spray the unmarked side of the cardboard with spray adhesive. Position the embossed mulberry paper wrong side down over the cardboard. Place a sheet of blank newsprint over the paper and use the flat edge of the bone folder to burnish it to the cardboard. Turn the cardboard over and trim away the excess mulberry paper with the craft knife by aligning the edge of the ruler with the edge of the cardboard. (See photo below.)
7. Score the folds by aligning the ruler with each score line, then lightly running the pointed edge of the bone folder along the ruler's edge. Erase the pencil lines.
8. Crease the folds along the score lines and assemble the box by applying white glue to the flaps.
9. Insert the stationery into the box and tie it with the jute string.

FERN FRAME AND GIFT WRAP

As in the boxed stationery set on pages 94–95, graceful fern fronds and lush greens play a prominent role in this project, though here green serves as a backdrop for striking yet elegant gold-embossed ferns.

The 6½- × 8½-inch (16.5- × 21.6-cm) wooden frame used in this project, which has a 3- × 5-inch (7.6- × 12.7-cm) window, was purchased already finished. (Keep in mind that embossing on finished wood takes longer than it does on paper, and that the embossing tool must be kept moving at all times to prevent scorching the surface.) Complete the theme by wrapping your beautiful frame in maidenhair fern gift wrap. As a finishing touch, trim the package with gold ribbon.

MATERIALS
Project
Green wooden frame with gift wrap
Stamps
For the frame
Monkey fern (A1102E)
For the gift wrap
Maidenhair fern (A1129E)
Inks and Embossing Powders
Embossing ink stamp pad
Gold embossing powder
Papers and Wrapping Supplies
Green mulberry paper
Gold ribbon
Miscellaneous
Dust cloth
Small paint brush
Embossing heat tool
Scissors
Double-stick tape

FRAME

1. Wipe the surface of the frame with a clean dust cloth to remove dust and any body oils.
2. Ink the monkey fern stamp with embossing ink, then stamp it on the lower right-hand corner of the frame. If the frame's finish is glossy, "kiss" the die to the wood to prevent the stamp from slipping.
3. Sprinkle the print with gold embossing powder, then tap off the excess. Remove any stray flecks of powder with a clean small paint brush. Use the embossing heat tool to melt the embossing powder. To avoid scorching the surface of the frame, keep moving the heat tool over the image, and do not apply heat to areas of the image that have already melted.
4. Repeat steps 2 and 3 to stamp and emboss two more ferns on the frame: one on the lower third of the left-hand border, and another roughly in the center of the top border. (See photo below.)

GIFT WRAP

1. Cut a piece of mulberry paper so that it's large enough to wrap either the frame itself or its gift box.
2. Ink the maidenhair fern stamp with embossing ink, then stamp an image on the paper. Re-ink the stamp to make three or four more prints.
3. Sprinkle all the prints with gold embossing powder. Tap off the excess, then remove stray flecks with a small paint brush. Save time by applying heat to three or four images at a time instead of embossing each individual fern. Continue stamping and embossing the images until the entire sheet of gift wrap is complete.
4. Wrap the frame or the gift box with the gift wrap so that the seams are on the back, then seal them with double-stick tape. Trim the package with gold ribbon.

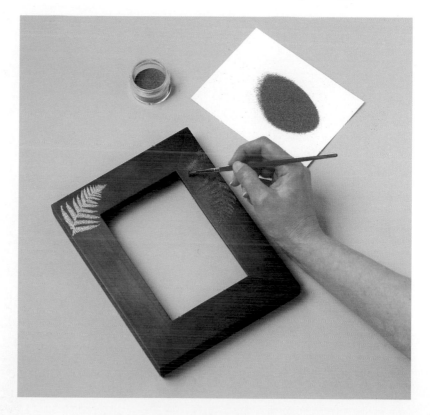

JAPANESE JOURNAL

Give an artist or a writer a special place to compose creative thoughts and experimental sketches—a beautiful handmade journal. This project provides a primer in bookbinding techniques, including creating a cover and making a simple grommet binding. The front cover features Japanese *mon*–style motifs in a color scheme of lavender and black with touches of gold.

To find bookbinding supplies in your area, check your phone directory under "Bookbinding Supplies and Equipment."

MATERIALS

Stamps
Bamboo and shell stamps from the Japanese art collection (760.02)

Inks and Embossing Powders
Black pigment ink stamp pad

Gold metallic pigment ink stamp pad

Gold embossing powder

Papers
Two 7 1/2- × 6 1/4-inch (19 × 16-cm) and two 1- × 6 1/4-inch (2.5- × 16-cm) pieces of stiff cardboard

Two 9 1/4- × 8-inch (23.6- × 20.3-cm) and two 7- × 5 3/4-inch (17.8- × 14.6 cm) pieces of lavender mulberry paper

1 3/4-inch (4.5-cm) square of gold crinkled paper

1 1/2-inch (3.8-cm) square of black paper

20 sheets of sketch paper cut to 8 1/2 × 6 inches (21.6 × 15.2 cm)

Binding Supplies
Two 4 1/4- × 8-inch (10.8- × 20.3-cm) pieces of black bookbinding cloth

Bookbinding glue

Paint brush (to apply the glue)

Grommet tool

Gold grommets

15 inches (38 cm) of black cord

Thin gold cording (optional)

Miscellaneous
Spray adhesive

Gold metallic pen

Hole punch

1. Use black pigment ink to stamp the large pieces of mulberry paper with the bamboo stamp in a dense, random pattern. (See Photo 1.) Let dry.

2. To prepare the covers, lightly spray adhesive on the unstamped side of one of the pieces of mulberry paper. Center one of the large pieces of cardboard over the paper, then press down firmly. Trim 1/2 inch (1.3 cm) of overhang from the top and bottom edges of the paper, then fold back the two side pieces, the top piece, then the bottom piece onto the cardboard. (See Photo 2.) Repeat with the other large piece of cardboard and stamped mulberry paper.

3. Fold one piece of bookbinding cloth in half lengthwise, wrong sides together, then crease the fold. Unfold it and apply bookbinding glue to the wrong side. With the cloth right side down, position the long edge of one of the cardboard strips against the crease of the fold, then place one of the covers, face down, about 1/8 inch (0.32 cm) from the other long edge of the strip. Fold the top and bottom edges of the cloth down over the strip and cover. (See Photo 3.) Apply more glue to the left side of the cloth, then fold it over onto the strip and cover. Repeat with the other piece of bookbinding cloth, cardboard strip, and cover.

4. Lightly spray adhesive on the wrong sides of the two smaller pieces of mulberry paper, then affix one to the inside of each cover.

5. Press two grommets through the center of each strip of cardboard about 1 1/2 inches (3.8 cm) from the top and bottom edges. (See Photo 4.)

6. Glue the square of gold paper on the diagonal near the bottom right-hand corner of the front cover. Carefully outline the edges of the black paper square with the gold metallic pen. Use gold ink to stamp the shell stamp in the center of the black square, then emboss it with gold embossing powder. Glue the black square over the gold one.

7. Punch holes in the sketch paper so that they line up with the grommets in the cover. Sandwich the paper between the front and back covers and lace the cord through the holes. Fasten it with a square knot at the top. For an additional decorative touch, wrap the ends of the black cord with thin gold cording.

1

2

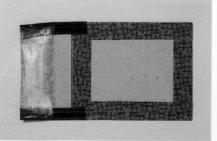

3

4

BORDER-PATTERN T-SHIRT

By using rubber stamps, fabric inks and paints, and small rhinestones, you can transform a plain T-shirt into a richly patterned work of wearable art. This gift is just right for the friend who yearns to look special but hates getting dressed up, or someone who loves wearing one-of-a-kind garments. For tips and ideas for other T-shirt designs, refer to the Variations box on the opposite page.

MATERIALS
Project
Cream-colored cotton
T-shirt
Stamps
Ornamental square
(A414C)
Diamond (A413C)
Inks and Fabric Paints
Black dye-based ink
stamp pad
Violet fabric ink stamp
pad
Royal blue fabric ink
stamp pad
Gold metallic dimensional
fabric paint
Embellishments
Blue and purple
rhinestones
Miscellaneous
Blank newsprint
Scrap paper
Scissors
Stamp positioning tool
Tracing paper
Stamp cleaner
Paper towels
Fabric glue

1. Wash the T-shirt to remove sizing, then dry and iron as directed on the label. To prevent ink bleed-through, insert one or two sheets of blank newsprint inside the T-shirt.
2. Using black dye-based ink, stamp several prints of both images on scrap paper. Let dry, then cut the prints out and lay them directly on the T-shirt to determine the amount of space between each element. (The spacing and number of stamped elements per row will depend on the size of your T-shirt.) Start by placing the center motif in each row, then position the first and last motifs in each row. Complete the rows by positioning the remaining motifs between the center and end motifs, leaving a consistent amount of space in between. (See Photo 1.)
3. Using the stamp positioning tool, black dye-based ink, and tracing paper, create a tracing-paper template for each of the images. Clean the stamps thoroughly with stamp cleaner and paper towels.
4. Place one of the tracing-paper templates over a corresponding scrap-paper print. Align the corner of the stamp positioning tool with the corner of the template, then remove both the template and the scrap-paper print. Ink the stamp with the violet fabric ink, aligning its block with the corner of the stamp positioning tool. Stamp one color at a time, starting with the violet. (See Photo 2.) Repeat this step for the prints stamped in royal blue.
5. Allow the inks to dry, then remove the newsprint. If necessary, heat-set the inks on the reverse side of the fabric as indicated in the manufacturer's instructions.
6. Insert a clean sheet of blank newsprint into the T-shirt. Use the dimensional paint to add arrow designs between the stamped images and to accent the diamond stamps with dots. (See Photo 3.) Let dry.
7. Use the fabric glue to affix a purple or blue rhinestone to the center of each ornamental square. Allow the T-shirt to dry overnight.

VARIATIONS
Give your friend an
expression of your
creativity by experimenting
with color and design:
• Use geometric stamp
  images as patterns for
  applying dimensional
  paints.
• Use puff paint to
  accent your designs.
• For a simple yet
  sophisticated look,
  stamp a dark-color shirt
  with black fabric ink.

1

2

3

RECIPE BOX GIFT SET

In this project—an excellent gift for an enthusiastic home cook—watercolors, rubber stamps, and colored pencils are used to make a cheerful assortment of kitchen accessories. In addition to the recipe box and matching recipe cards, you can create a personalized label for a recipe journal and some gift tags to encourage your friend to share the fruits of her bounty. Use the box designs shown below and on the opposite page, as well as the sample card, label, and gift tag designs on page 104, as the basis for your own gift set. Experiment with different patterns and color combinations on scrap paper before getting started. Above all, don't try to paint perfect squares of color. Much of the charm of this style of design is its handmade look.

You can find paper-covered boxes at many art supply and craft stores, or you can make them yourself.

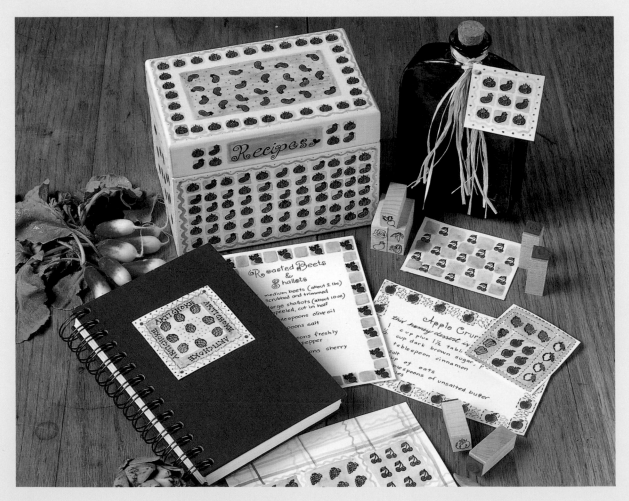

MATERIALS

Project
Paper-covered box with recipe cards, labels, and gift tags

Stamps
Petite fruits (740.03) and vegetables (740.04)

Inks
Black pigment ink stamp pad

Papers
White postcards

Paints, Pencils, and Markers
Watercolors in assorted colors

Watercolor brush

Fine-point markers (in colors to coordinate with watercolors)

Colored pencils in assorted colors

Black permanent fine-point marker

RECIPE BOX

1. Leaving enough space to accommodate a narrow decorative border (see step 2), use watercolors to paint blocks of color approximately ½ inch (1.3 cm) square on the front of the recipe box. Allow the paints to dry thoroughly.
2. Add an interesting border with your watercolors, such as a squiggly line or a zigzag. Add random dots with a fine-point marker.
3. Stamp fruits and vegetables with black pigment ink over the watercolor blocks. Allow the ink to dry thoroughly before coloring the images with colored pencils.
4. In the center of the front of the lid, paint a block of color large enough to accommodate the word "Recipes," then paint four smaller blocks of color on either side of it. Let dry thoroughly. Stamp fruits and vegetables with black pigment ink in the small blocks, and let dry before coloring with colored pencils. Write "Recipes" in the center of the large color block with a black permanent marker.
5. Paint a large block of color in the center of each side of the box. Let dry, then paint a border similar to the one on the front of the box. Randomly stamp fruits and vegetables in the center of the color block with black pigment ink. Let dry before coloring with colored pencils. Add random dots to the border with a fine-point marker.
6. Leaving enough space around the edge of the lid top to accommodate the narrow border used on the front and sides of the box, paint ½-inch (1.3-cm) blocks of color around the perimeter of the lid top. Let dry. Paint the remaining space in the center of the lid top with a single large block of color, let dry, then add the border around the edge.
7. Using black pigment ink, randomly stamp fruits and vegetables within the large block of color, as well as on each of the ½-inch (1.3-cm) watercolor blocks. Allow the ink to dry before coloring the stamps with colored pencils. Add dots to the border and around the stamps in the large center block with a fine-point marker.

A sample design for the recipe box.

103

RECIPE CARDS, LABELS, AND GIFT TAGS

1. Paint ½-inch (1.3-cm) blocks of color around the border of the postcard. Let dry.
2. Stamp the images over alternate squares with black pigment ink. Allow the ink to dry before coloring the images with colored pencils.
3. If desired, add dots, lines, or borders with fine-point markers.
4. For the recipe cards, use the black marker to write the ingredients list in the center of the card, then write the recipe on the back.

Sample designs for a recipe card, recipe journal labels, and a gift tag.

Roasted Beets & Shallots

7 medium beets (about 2 lbs) scrubbed and trimmed

10 large shallots (about 10 oz) unpeeled, cut in half

2 tablespoons olive oil

1½ teaspoons salt

3/8 tea spoons freshly ground pepper

1½ tablespoons sherry vinegar

CELESTIAL TREASURE BOX AND GIFT TAG

This gold-embossed wooden box with whimsical ball-shaped feet and lid handle provides an elegant place to store heavenly treasures. Since the design of this project is far more precise than the Recipe Box Gift Set (pages 102–104), you'll need to use a stamp positioning tool, which can be awkward on a three-dimensional surface. In addition, stamping on a small curved surface can be a little tricky, so you might prefer to work on a box with a flat lid. Practicing the technique (see step 7) and organizing all your materials beforehand will make things run more smoothly.

MATERIALS
Project
Unfinished wood box with hinged lid (with five 1-inch wood knobs)
Stamps
Eight-point star (A1054C)
Star trio (A1055C)
Moon (A929E)
Swirls (A952E)
Inks and Embossing Powders
Black dye-based ink stamp pad
Embossing ink stamp pad
Gold embossing powder
Paints
Blue acrylic
Gold metallic acrylic
Brushes
Two acrylic paint brushes
Small paint brush (to brush off excess embossing powder)
Papers
Gold crinkled paper
Blue handmade paper with gold threads
Miscellaneous
Fine sandpaper
Tack cloth
Tracing paper
Stamp positioning tool
Stamp cleaner
Paper towels
Low-adhesive paper tape
Embossing heat tool
Wood glue
Ripple-pattern scissors (M9204)
Scissors
Star hole punch
Glue stick
9 inches (22.9 cm) of thin gold cord

SURFACE PREPARATION

1. If necessary, sand the box in the direction of the wood grain until smooth, then wipe it lightly with tack cloth to remove all sanding dust.
2. Paint the box with blue acrylic paint. Paint the wood knobs with two coats of gold acrylic paint. (See Photo 1.) Let dry.

STAMPING AND EMBOSSING

3. Using the black dye-based ink, the tracing paper, and the stamp positioning tool, prepare templates for all four of the stamps. Clean the stamps with stamp cleaner and paper towels.
4. To keep the lid in place while stamping and embossing, tape it closed with a small piece of low-adhesive paper tape. Position the template for the eight-point star so that it's centered on the front of the box. Align the right-angle corner of the stamp positioning tool with the corner of the template. Leaving the positioning tool in place, remove the template, then ink the eight-point star stamp with embossing ink and stamp it by aligning it with the corner of the tool.
5. Sprinkle the stamped image with gold embossing powder, then tap off any excess. Use a small paint brush to remove any stray flecks of powder. Use the embossing tool to melt the powder. (See Photo 2.)
6. Repeat steps 4 and 5 to stamp and emboss four more eight-point stars: two on the front of the box, each centered within the space between the first star and the edge of the box; and one on each side, which should also be centered.
7. Stamp and emboss the star trio in the top right- and left-hand corners of the lid top, then stamp it again on the lower right-hand side, slightly toward the center. If you're working on a curved top, stamp the images by carefully pressing down on the lower part of the stamp, then roll upward onto the curve while exerting pressure slightly.
8. Stamp and emboss the moon on the lower left-hand side of the lid top, rolling the stamp from bottom to top as explained in step 7.
9. Use paper tape to mask the front, sides, and back of the box. Ink the swirls stamp with embossing ink, stamp the far left-hand area of each side of the lid, then emboss with gold embossing powder. (See Photo 3.) Use the template for the swirl stamp and the stamp positioning tool to align the next print so that it merges with the one to its left. Stamp and emboss the swirls until all four sides of the lid are complete. Remove the paper tape.

FINISHING

10. Glue a gold knob to each of the bottom four corners of the box with wood glue. Let dry.
11. Glue a gold knob to the center of the lid top. Let dry. (See Photo 4.)

GIFT TAG

1. Using the ripple-pattern scissors, cut a 3-inch (7.6-cm) square from the gold paper.
2. Cut a 2³⁄₄-inch (7-cm) square from the blue paper with the straight-edge scissors.
3. Ink the moon stamp with embossing ink and stamp it in the center of the blue square. Sprinkle it with gold embossing powder, then melt it with the embossing heat tool. Use the hole punch to punch several stars around the moon.
4. Glue the stamped blue square to the center of the gold square.
5. Punch a star in the top left corner of the tag and thread it with the gold cord.

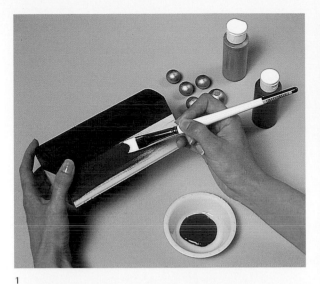

1

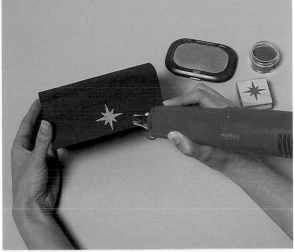

2

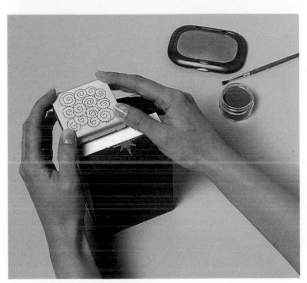

3

4

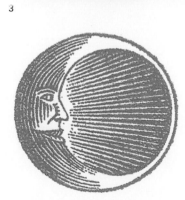

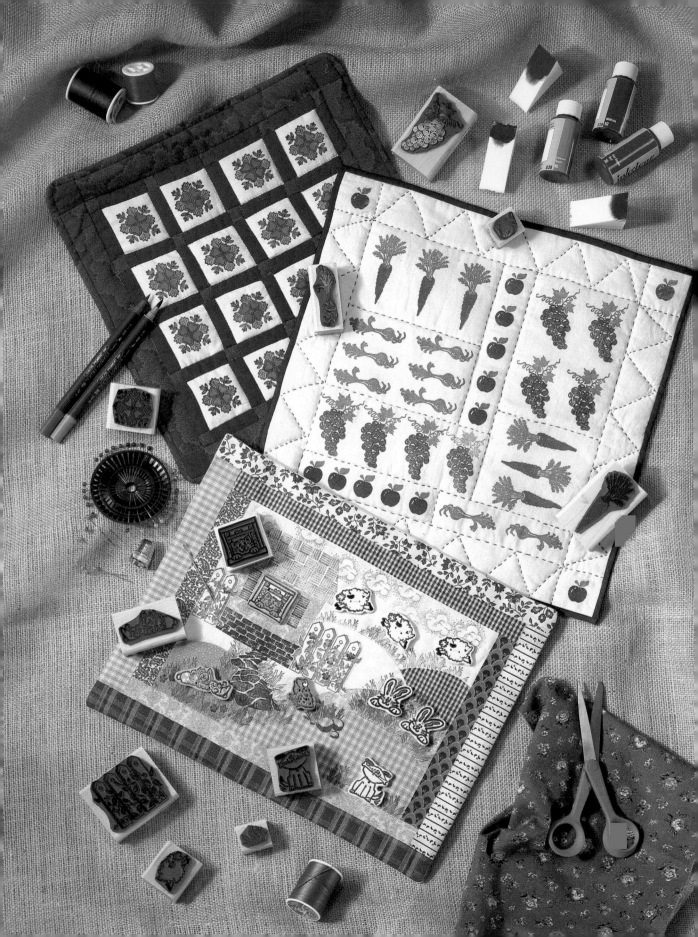

STAMPING FOR STITCHERS

Fabrics have been embellished with paints and inks since civilization began. Rubber stamping is simply the latest advancement in an ancient craft. In this chapter, the tools of the rubber stamper are combined with those of the stitcher to create beautiful pillows, quilts, and wall hangings. It's important to note that these techniques can also be used to stamp coordinating decorative items, and easily adapted for apparel. If you're new to sewing, keep in mind that a piece of fabric holds the same decorative potential as a sheet of paper.

LINEN AND LACE VICTORIAN POSY PILLOW

Throughout history, flowers have been ascribed symbolic significance. The Victorians in particular were noted for their complex floral iconography, which was often expressed in small nosegays or posies that were given as gifts. The word "posy" itself has a dual meaning, referring to a brief poetic sentiment as well as a small bouquet of flowers.

The pink rose posy featured on this pillow signifies "perfect happiness," making it an auspicious addition to your home's decor. To accentuate the stamp's antique look, we used a square of vintage lace recycled from an old doily, but contemporary lace would work just as well. The pillow's finished dimensions are 11³/₄ inches (29.9 cm) square.

MATERIALS

Stamps

Beatrice's butterfly posy (A337G)

Cynthia's lace stripe (A339F)

Inks

Black dye-based ink stamp pad

Chocolate brown fabric ink stamp pad

Translucent Fabric Paints

Terracotta

Green

Lavender

Fabrics

Note: All dimensions include ¹⁄₄-inch (0.64-cm) seam allowance

One 6-inch (15.2-cm) square of cotton

Broad-openwork lace trim

Two 12 inch (30.5-cm) squares of linen

Sewing Supplies

Thread (in colors to match the linen and the lace)

Polyester fiberfill

Miscellaneous

Tracing paper

Stamp positioning tool

Stamp cleaner

Paper towels

Small paint brush

1. Except for the lace, wash, dry, and press the fabrics.

2. Using black dye-based ink, the tracing paper, and the stamp positioning tool, prepare tracing-paper templates for both stamps. Clean the stamps with stamp cleaner and paper towels.

3. Position the tracing-paper template for the lace stripe stamp at an angle over one of the corners of the square of cotton fabric. Align the right-angle corner of the stamp positioning tool with the corner of the template. Leaving the stamp positioning tool in place, remove the template, then ink the lace stripe stamp with brown fabric ink and stamp it by aligning its block with the corner of the positioning tool. Repeat for the three remaining corners. (See Photo 1.)

4. Position the template for the posy stamp in the center of the stamped cotton square. Align the right-angle corner of the stamp positioning tool with the corner of the template, remove the template, then ink the posy stamp with brown fabric ink and stamp it in the center of the square by aligning it with the corner of the positioning tool.

5. Allow the ink to dry. If necessary, heat-set the ink on the reverse side of the fabric as indicated in the manufacturer's instructions.

6. Using a small paint brush, color the images with translucent fabric paints. If needed, use the color indexes on the stamp blocks as guides to your color choices. (See Photo 2.) Let dry. Heat-set the paints if necessary.

7. Using a buttonhole stitch, sew the lace trim around the perimeter of the stamped cotton square while stitching the square to the center of the right side of one of the linen squares. If necessary, tack down the edges of the lace to keep it from hanging loosely.

8. Place the two linen squares right sides together. Stitch the edges of pillow together, leaving a 3-inch (7.6-cm) opening through which the polyester fiberfill can be inserted.

9. Turn the pillow right side out and stuff it with fiberfill. Slipstitch the opening closed.

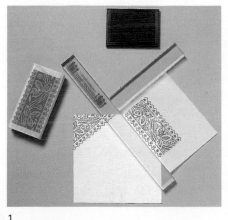

1

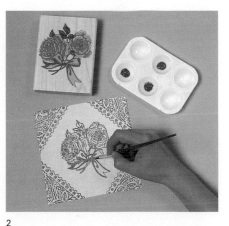

2

QUILTED GARDEN WALL HANGING

Whether they cultivate a few herbs in a windowbox or an abundance of produce on several acres, home cooks love to prepare and serve the harvest of their own gardens. This stamped and hand-quilted wall hanging, whose finished measurements are 13½ inches (34.3 cm) square, makes a charming kitchen accessory for a gardener, or for anyone who simply appreciates the beauty of fruits and vegetables. For other kitchen decorating ideas, refer to the Variations box on the opposite page.

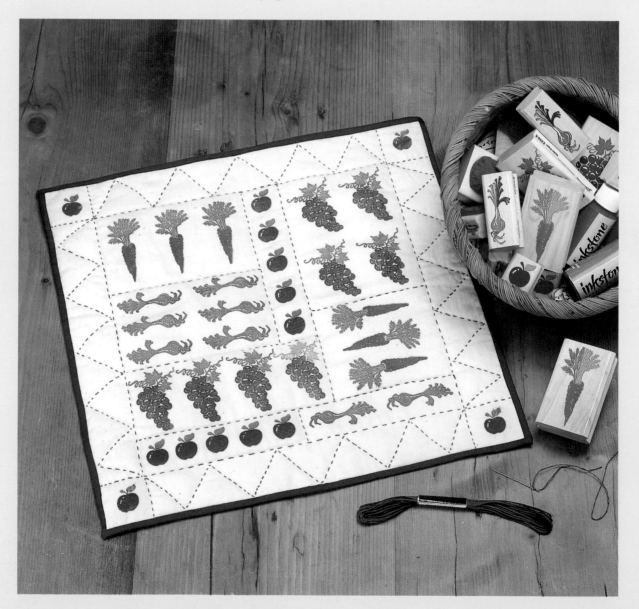

MATERIALS

Quilting Diagram
Page 151

Stamps
Crunchy carrot (Z585E)
Little apple (Z160A)
Garden grapes (Z356E)
Chef's shallot (Z584C)

Inks
Black dye-based ink
stamp pad
Fabric inks
Orange
Emerald green
Red
Purple

Fabrics
Two 13½-inch (34.3-cm)
squares of muslin
One 13½-inch (34.3-cm)
square of thin,
lightweight batting

Sewing Supplies
Removable fabric
marking pen
Dark green thread
Single-fold bias tape
Dark green embroidery
floss
Embroidery needle

Miscellaneous
Scissors
Ruler
Scrap paper
Tracing paper
Stamp positioning tool
Stamp cleaner
Paper towels
Four wedge-shaped
foam sponges (one for
each color of fabric ink)

VARIATIONS

- Use one of the stamps to create all-over patterned napkins and placemats.
- Stamp the walls with a matching frieze or chair rail border.
- For a dimensional look, stamp Creative Paperclay to make buttons, then sew them on the wall hanging. See the Clay Button Wall Hanging project, pages 121–123, for instructions.

1. Wash, dry, and press the muslin.
2. On the right side of one of the muslin squares, use the fabric marking pen to mark off rectangles with a dashed line according to the diagram on page 151.
3. Using black dye-based ink, stamp three carrots, five apples, four grapes, and six shallots on scrap paper. Cut the prints out and set them aside.
4. Use black dye-based ink and the stamp positioning tool to prepare a single tracing-paper template containing all four stamps. (See Photo 1.) Clean the stamps with stamp cleaner and paper towels.
5. Place the carrot prints on the muslin in the upper left-hand rectangle. Use foam sponges to ink the carrot stamp with the orange and green fabric inks. (See Photo 2.)
6. Place the template for the carrot stamp over one of the prints. Align the corner of the positioning tool with the corner of the template. Leaving the positioning tool in place, remove both the template and the print. Stamp the carrot stamp on the muslin by aligning its block with the corner of the positioning tool. Repeat for the two remaining carrot prints. (See Photo 3.)
7. Repeat steps 5 and 6 for the other stamps until each rectangle and all four corners have been stamped. Let dry for 24 hours, then heat-set the inks as indicated in the manufacturer's instructions if required.
8. In the border surrounding the stamped rectangles, use the ruler and the fabric marking pen to mark off five equilateral triangles on each side and squares in each corner with dashed lines.
9. Press the top and the backing, then sandwich the batting between the wrong sides of the muslin. Pin the sandwich at several points to keep the layers from slipping. Sew the bias tape binding to each side, then to the top and bottom. Fold the extra stub of binding around each corner on the back, then sew it in place.
10. Use the embroidery floss to quilt running stitches over the dashed fabric-marker lines. Follow the manufacturer's instructions to remove the marker.

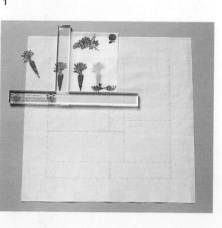

1

2

3

MINIATURE PIECED QUILT

This delightful miniature quilt can serve as a wall hanging, a doll's lap quilt, or an infant's coverlet. Select the fabrics first, then purchase fabric inks and textile markers to match the fabrics, mixing colors if necessary. Purple and magenta were used in this project, but you can color the quilt stamp with any color scheme.

The amount of materials you'll need to purchase will depend on the size of the quilt you want to make. To make the quilt shown below, the image was stamped on 2½-inch (6.4-cm) squares and assembled with 1- × 2½-inch (2.5- × 6.4-cm) sashes and 1-inch (2.5-cm) square posts, all including a ¼-inch (0.32-cm) seam allowance. To create a larger quilt, stamp additional squares, or increase the size of the squares and use a larger stamp.

MATERIALS

Stamps
Floral quilt (A902C)

Inks
Black fabric ink stamp pad

Textile Markers
Pink
Turquoise
Light violet

Fabrics
Muslin (on which to stamp the image)
Purple floral print fabric (for the posts, border, binding, and backing)
Magenta floral print fabric (for the sashes and border posts)
Thin, lightweight batting

Stitching Supplies
Thread (to match the color of the backing)

Miscellaneous
Scissors

1. Except for the batting, wash, dry, and press the fabrics.
2. Based on the projected size of your quilt, choose the dimensions of your quilt squares, then cut the appropriate number of squares from the muslin. Using these dimensions as your guide, cut the sashes, posts, border, border posts, and binding from the other two fabrics.
3. Ink the quilt stamp with black fabric ink, then stamp it in the center of one of the muslin squares. (See Photo 1.) Re-inking the stamp after making each print, stamp the remaining squares. Allow the ink to dry.
4. Color the stamped images with textile markers, alternating the colors of the motifs in an equal number of blocks. (See Photo 2.) If necessary, heat-set the inks as indicated in the manufacturer's instructions.
5. Arrange the stamped squares, sashes, and posts in the intended layout. Using a 1/4-inch (0.64-cm) seam allowance, pin, then sew, the first row of horizontal sashes and posts together, then the first row of vertical sashes and stamped quilt blocks. As you complete each row, remove the pins and press the seam allowances toward the darker of the two fabrics. Pin, piece, and press horizontal rows until you complete the last row of posts and sashes.
6. Pin and sew the horizontal seams of the first two horizontal rows, remove the pins, then press the seams. Repeat this step for the remaining horizontal rows, the borders, and the border posts.
7. Cut the backing and batting about 1 inch (2.5 cm) larger on all sides than the pieced top. Press the top, the backing, and the batting, layer them to create the sandwich, then pin it at several points to keep the layers from slipping.
8. Machine-quilt the sandwich using the "stitch in the ditch" pattern. (The ditches are the little valleys between pieces formed by the seam lines.) Removing the pins as you work, sew the first quilting line near the center of the quilt, from the lower edge of the top border to the upper edge of the bottom border, then sew the remaining vertical seam lines.
9. Starting at the center, quilt the horizontal seam lines from border to border. Quilt the inner edge of the border, then each square, post, and sash. Trim the edges of the sandwich so that all the layers are even.
10. Pin the binding to the top edge of the quilt top, right sides together, then sew them together 1/4 inch (0.64 cm) from the edge. Trim the ends of the binding so that they're even with the ends of the quilt. Repeat this step for the opposite edge of the quilt.
11. Remove the pins, then turn the binding under so that it covers any raw edges. Hand-sew the binding to the backing on each side of the quilt.
12. Repeat steps 10 and 11 for the other two sides of the quilt.

1

2

PRIMITIVE ART WALL HANGING

Travelers often collect unusual artifacts that reflect the diversity of the countries they've visited and the creativity of the cultures they've observed. The 16½- × 15½-inch (41.9- × 39.4-cm) wall hanging shown below, which includes stamp images that are rendered in graphic styles reminiscent of those indigenous to Africa and Australia, would complement such a collection perfectly. The images are stamped in black on a monochromatic color scheme consisting of two rich earth tones and a neutral beige and embellished with buttons and beads made from bone, pearl, stone, and wood.

MATERIALS
Piecing Diagram
Page 152
Stamps
Zebra stencil (A417D)
Diamond (A413C)
Serpent (A412C)
Tribal mask (A428D)
Giraffe print (A853E)
Spiral gecko (A419C)
Split diamond (A416C)
Gazelle (A411D)

Inks
Black dye-based ink
stamp pad
Black fabric ink stamp
pad

Fabrics
1/4 yard (9- × 45-inch
[22.9- × 114.3-cm] piece)
of beige cotton fabric
1/3 yard (12- × 45-inch
[30.5- × 114.3-cm] piece)
of rust cotton fabric
1/4 yard (9- × 45-inch
[22.9- × 114.3-cm] piece)
of saffron cotton fabric
1/2 yard (18- × 45-inch
[38.1- × 40.6-cm] piece) of
thin, lightweight batting
1/2 yard (18- × 45-inch
[38.1- × 40.6-cm] piece)
of black cotton fabric

Stitching Supplies
Black embroidery floss
Rust embroidery floss
One package of 1/2-inch
(1.3-cm) black bias binding

Embellishments
Assorted bone and pearl
buttons
Assorted stone and
wooden beads

Miscellaneous
Stamp positioning tool
Tracing paper
Scrap paper
Scissors
Stamp cleaner
Paper towels

1. Except for the batting, wash, dry, and press the fabrics.
2. Refer to the diagram on page 152 for piece measurements. Add 1/4-inch (0.64-cm) seam allowance to all sides of each piece when cutting.
3. Using black dye-based ink, tracing paper, and the stamp positioning tool, create tracing-paper templates for each of the stamp images.
4. Using black dye-based ink, stamp five zebras, eleven diamonds, six serpents, three tribal masks, five giraffe-skin prints, four spiral geckos, eight split diamonds, and two gazelles on scrap paper, then cut them out. Clean the stamps with stamp cleaner and paper towels.
5. Lay out the scrap-paper prints on each of the fabric pieces. (See Photo 1.) The spacing of the elements will depend on the size and number of embellishments you plan to use on each piece.
6. Place a tracing-paper template over one of its corresponding scrap-paper prints. Align the corner of the positioning tool with the corner of the template. Leaving the positioning tool in place, remove both the template and the print. Ink the image with black fabric ink, then stamp it by aligning the corner of its block with the corner of the tool. (See Photo 2.) Re-inking the stamp to make each print, repeat until all the fabric pieces are stamped.
7. Allow the ink to dry. If necessary, heat-set the ink.
8. Pin, piece, and press the stamped pieces of fabric as per the diagram on page 152.
9. Cut pieces of batting and black fabric (for the backing) the same size as the pieced top, then press them. Layer the batting between the wrong sides of the pieced top and the backing, then pin the sandwich at several points to keep the layers from slipping.
10. Pin the binding to the top edge of the quilt top right sides together, then sew them 1/4 inch (0.64 cm) from the edge. Trim the ends of the binding so that they're even with the ends of the quilt. Repeat for the opposite edge of the quilt.
11. Remove the pins, then turn the binding under so that it covers any raw edges. Hand-sew the binding to the backing on each side of the quilt.
12. Repeat steps 10 and 11 for the other two sides of the quilt.
13. Embellish the quilt with embroidery floss, buttons, and beads, using them to balance prints that were stamped off-center, either intentionally or unintentionally.

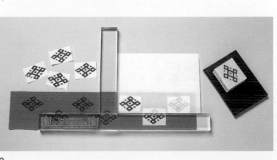

1

2

COUNTING SHEEP PILLOW

Stamped in tranquil pastels, this fun, fanciful pillow can lure even the most restless youngster to dreams of peaceful slumber, and can help teach him or her how to count. Showcase your child's special pillow by propping it on the rocking chair you both share during story time, or on his or her own little armchair. For suggestions on stamping coordinating pieces, both for apparel and home decor, see the Variations box on the opposite page.

MATERIALS

Flange Patterns
Page 153

Stamps
Square, triangle, and heart stamps from the Petite basic shapes collection (740.01)
Jumping sheep (735C)

Inks
Black dye-based ink stamp pad
Fabric ink stamp pads
Sky blue
Lavender
Medium pink
Turquoise

Textile Markers
Green
Pink

Fabrics
½ yard (18- × 45-inch [38.1- × 40.6-cm] piece) of white cotton sheeting
¼ yard (9- × 45-inch [22.9- × 114.3-cm] piece) of light blue cotton sheeting

Stitching Supplies
Removable fabric marking pen
Light blue thread
Polyester fiberfill

Miscellaneous
Scissors
Scrap paper
Ruler
Pencil
Stamp cleaner
Paper towels

Optional
Stamp positioning tool
Tracing paper

VARIATIONS

Kids—and many adults—love coordinating themes:

• Stamp an oversize T-shirt to wear as pajamas.

• Design a complete bedroom decor by stamping the same patterns on sheets, curtains, and walls.

To add another "dimension," paint the sheep with white puff paint.

1. Wash, dry, and press the fabrics.

2. Cut two 14-inch (35.6-cm) squares of white cotton sheeting. (All fabric measurements include ¼-inch [0.64-cm] seam allowance.)

3. Use a ruler and pencil to draw an 11-inch (27.9-cm) line in the center of a 2- × 12-inch (5- × 30.5-cm) strip of scrap paper. Ink the square stamp with black dye-based ink and, starting at the left end of the line, stamp it so that the bottom of the square sits on the line. Re-ink the stamp, then stamp the next print so that its top aligns with the line and its upper left-hand corner meets the lower right-hand corner of the first print. Continue inking and stamping in this manner to create a checkerboard border. Repeat this step to create two more checkerboard borders, as well as two similar-style borders with the triangle stamp. (If you have access to a photocopier, simply stamp one of each border and make two copies of the checkerboard border and one of the triangle border.)

4. Position the checkerboard and triangle scrap-paper borders on the right side of one of the cotton squares. Refer to Photo 1 for placement and use a ruler to ensure that the spacing between the borders is equal.

5. Use the fabric marking pen to mark points on the fabric at the ends of each border. Remove the paper pattern and use the ruler and fabric marking pen to make a straight line connecting the two dots. (See Photo 2.) Repeat this step for the four remaining borders.

6. To stamp a checkerboard border, position one of paper patterns slightly below one of the marker lines. Stamp the top row of squares with sky blue fabric ink, using the line as a guide for alignment and the paper pattern as a guide for spacing between squares, then stamp the bottom row. Repeat this step to stamp the two remaining checkerboard borders.

7. To stamp the two triangle borders, repeat step 5 using lavender fabric ink for the top rows of triangles and pink fabric ink for the bottom rows. Clean the square and triangle stamps with stamp cleaner and paper towels.

8. Use the black dye-based ink to stamp sixteen sheep on scrap paper. Cut the prints out and set them aside. Clean the stamp with stamp cleaner and paper towels.

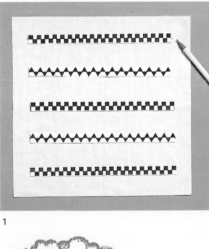

1

2

9. Position the scrap-paper sheep prints on the fabric. (See Photo 3.) Ink the sheep stamp with turquoise fabric ink. Position the inked stamp over one of the prints, then remove the pattern before stamping directly on the fabric. (For precise positioning, use a stamp positioning tool and tracing-paper template.) Re-inking the stamp before making each print, repeat until all the sheep have been stamped.

10. Ink the heart stamp with pink fabric ink, then stamp it between two sheep. Continue inking and stamping to print one heart between each pair of sheep, as well as on both ends of each row. Use the green textile marker to draw a stem and leaves beneath each heart.

11. Use the pink fabric marker to add mini-dots in the white spaces between the squares of the blue checkerboard borders.

12. To make the triangle flanges, fold the blue cotton fabric in half lengthwise, right sides together. Align the base of the pattern (see page 153) with the crease of the fold, then cut the fabric to the pattern. Repeat this step to cut fifteen additional triangle flanges.

13. Keeping right sides together, stitch the two sides of one of the triangles closed. Clip the point of the triangle, turn it right side out, then press it with an iron. Repeat this step for the remaining triangles.

14. To make the four corner flanges, repeat steps 12 and 13 using the pattern on page 153. Once the corner flanges have all been pressed, baste them along the base, then pull the thread to shirr them into curves.

15. Baste the corner flanges to the right side of each of the four corners of the stamped square. Space the remaining triangles (four to a side) evenly between the corner flanges. With raw edges together, baste them into place.

16. Place the two squares right sides together. Stitch the edges of the pillow together, leaving a 3-inch (7.6-cm) opening through which the fiberfill can be inserted.

17. Turn the pillow right side out and press it. Stuff it with fiberfill and slipstitch the opening closed.

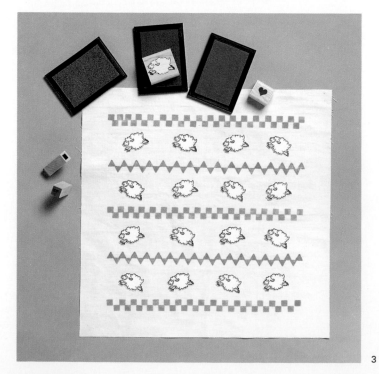

3

CLAY BUTTON WALL HANGING

By making buttons with Creative Paperclay™ and incorporating them into a fabric landscape, you can create a dimensional conversation piece for a child's room—an inventive way to use rubber stamps *and* fabric scraps. There's no need to limit your scenery or characters to what's shown in the example below. Create a backdrop for a beloved cartoon character, recreate an illustration from a favorite storybook, or collaborate with your child to weave an original yarn.

When adapting this project to fit a specific color scheme or fabric collection, select the inks to complement the colors of the fabrics. The dimensions of the wall hanging shown below are 11 × 14 inches (27.9 × 35.6 cm).

Pattern
Page 154
Stamps
For the wall hanging
Flagstone path (Z582E)
Line pattern from Petite basic shapes (740.01)
Posh picket (Z384E)
Patterned bricks (Z329C)
Cloud (Z327C)
Wild grass (Z310A)
Scattered flowers (Z033A)
Scattered stones (Z036C)
For the clay buttons
Jumping sheep (735C)
Bunny face (754C)
"Hello Kitty!" (759C)
Spike (A880C)
Toad (543C)
Flopsy, Mopsie & Cottontail (627D)
Inks
Black pigment ink stamp pad
Fabric ink stamp pads
Cornflower blue
Burgundy
Emerald green
Pine green
Royal blue
Fabrics
1/3 yard (12- × 45-inch [30.5- × 114.3-cm] piece) of muslin
1/3 yard of assorted print fabrics
1/3 yard (12- × 45-inch [30.5- × 114.3-cm] piece) thin, lightweight batting
Stitching Supplies
Double-sided fusible webbing
Cream-colored thread
Clay Button Supplies
One large package of Creative Paperclay
Butter knife
Toothpicks
Wax paper
Fine sandpaper
Acrylic paints (in assorted colors)
Assorted paint brushes
Gloss-finish water-based acrylic glaze
Miscellaneous
Scissors
Scrap paper

WALL HANGING

1. Wash, dry, and press the fabrics.
2. Enlarge the pattern by using one of the methods discussed on pages 146–147. Trace each piece onto scrap paper.
3. Determine which of the print fabrics will be used for each part of the pattern. Avoid busy prints for the pieces that will be stamped (see photo on the preceding page). Lay each piece of the pattern over the appropriate fabric and cut the pieces out. Following the manufacturer's instructions, iron fusible webbing to the wrong side of each of the fabric pieces.
4. For the border, cut two strips from your assorted print fabrics in each of the following dimensions (measurements include 1/4-inch [0.64-cm] seam allowance): 3/4 × 11 1/2 inches (1.91 × 29.2 cm); 3/4 × 14 1/2 inches (1.91 × 36.8 cm); 1 1/4 × 11 1/2 inches (3.2 × 29.2 cm); and 1 1/4 × 14 1/2 inches (3.2 × 36.8 cm). Iron fusible webbing to the wrong side of each piece.
5. Cut two pieces of muslin and one piece of batting, each measuring 11 1/2 × 14 1/2 inches (29.2 × 36.8 cm). Set aside one of the pieces of muslin and the batting.
6. On the right side of the other piece of muslin, arrange the pieces according to the pattern. Iron on the background pieces first, then overlap them with the foreground pieces. Slightly overlap the border pieces on top of the design. (See Photo 1.)
7. On scrap pieces of muslin or lightly patterned fabric, stamp the flagstone path in burgundy fabric ink, the line pattern for the roof in royal blue fabric ink, and picket fence in emerald green fabric ink. (See Photo 2. Note that some of the stamp images were isolated by means of selective inking.) Allow the ink to dry. Iron fusible webbing to the back of each piece, then cut the images out.
8. Ink the cat stamp with black pigment ink and stamp it on a piece of scrap paper. Cut the print out, then position it on the piece of fabric for the house. Use the line pattern stamp and the burgundy fabric ink to stamp the shutters on either side of the scrap-paper print. Remove the print, then stamp the bricks along the bottom of the house with burgundy ink. Allow the ink to dry.
9. Iron the house, roof, fence, and path into place.
10. Stamp the clouds, grass, flowers, and stones in appropriate colors, using the photo opposite as a guide to layout. Mask adjacent pieces of fabric as necessary. (See Photo 3.)
11. With the rights sides of the muslin together and the batting on the bottom, sew all four sides of the wall hanging, leaving a 6-inch (15.2-cm) opening. Trim the seams and clip the corners, then turn the hanging right side out. Slipstitch the opening closed and press the hanging flat.

CLAY BUTTONS

1. Roll the clay out on a smooth surface to 1/8-inch (0.32-cm) thickness.
2. Using black pigment ink, stamp three sheep, two bunny faces, and one cat, dog, toad, and group of bunnies each onto the clay.
3. Cut around the prints with a butter knife, leaving a small border around the outlines. (See Photo 4.) Pierce each one with a toothpick in two places to make buttonholes. Transfer the stamped clay to a sheet of wax paper and let dry overnight.
4. When the clay has dried completely, lightly sand any rough edges.
5. Paint each button with the acrylic paints. Let dry. (See Photo 5.)
6. To finish the buttons, apply an even coat of acrylic glaze. Let dry.
7. Sew the clay buttons into place on the wall hanging.

1

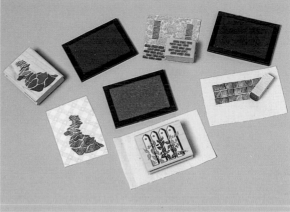

2

3

4

5

HOLIDAYS AND SPECIAL OCCASIONS

Creating beautiful correspondence or objects can make any occasion seem special. From designing cards and invitations for birthdays, bridal showers, Valentine's Day, Halloween, or New Year's Eve, to making elegant decorative items for Christmas or Hanukkah, rubber stamps can be used to commemorate significant events with imagination and artistry

BIRTHDAY PARTY ACCESSORIES

A kid's birthday party can be much more than cake, ice cream, and a quick round of "pin the tale on the donkey." Entice young guests with multicolored invitations, then organize a pre-party "stamping bee" to make matching hats that can be taken home as favors. While you teach the party-goers how to ink each element of a stamp with brush markers—and to clean the stamps whenever they want to use a new color—you'll be sure to infect them with your enthusiasm for stamping.

MATERIALS
Stamps
Icing on the cake (Z205E)
Candle city (Z206E)
Balloon (Z330B)
Birthday balloon (Z112C)
Party plans (Z588E)
Posh package (Z081C)
Party popper (Z425D)
Confetti (Z173C)
Party! (Z129D)
Happy birthday (Z065E)
Inks
Brush markers in assorted bright colors
Papers
For two invitations
One 11- × 17-inch (27.9- × 43.18-cm) piece of white, gloss-finish card stock
For the hats
A large roll of white, glossy coated gift wrap
Miscellaneous
Scissors
Stamp cleaner
Paper towels
Fine-tip markers in assorted colors
Ruler
For the invitations
Pencil
Craft knife
Foam dots
For the hats
Blank newsprint
Clear contact paper
Elastic cording
Stapler and staples

VARIATIONS
To make matching placemats, create a newsprint template, then use it to cut a placemat from the gift wrap. Outline the edges of the cut gift wrap with a brush marker. Ink the selected stamps with brush markers, then stamp them randomly on the placemat. Use fine-tip markers to add strings to the balloons. Cover both sides of the placemat with contact paper, then trim off any excess.

INVITATION

1. Cut a 4½- × 14½-inch (11.4- × 38.6-cm) piece from the card stock. Orient the card vertically, then draw a light pencil line across it 4¼ inches (10.8 cm) from the bottom.
2. Ink each element of the cake with a different brush marker, then remoisten the inks by breathing on the die. (Repeat after inking every stamp.) Stamp the cake on the card by aligning the top of it with the pencil line. Ink and stamp the candles on top of the cake.
3. Use the craft knife to die-cut the tops and sides of the candles. Create a mountain fold along the pencil line and pop the candles up. (See photo below.)
4. Make a valley fold 4¼ inches (10.8 cm) from the first. Fold the flap back over the candles so that about 1 inch (1.3 cm) covers their tops. Unfold the card.
5. Using both balloon stamps, stamp two uneven and overlapping rows of balloons across the top of the card. (As you change colors, clean the stamps with stamp cleaner and paper towels.) Die-cut the tops of the first row of balloons. Add strings to the balloons with the fine-tip markers.
6. Stamp the party plans stamp 1 inch (2.5 cm) below the second row of balloons. Use the fine-tip markers to add "fill-in" lines.
7. Stamp the central third of the card with packages, poppers, and both types of balloons. Stamp any blank areas in this area and on the front of the card with the confetti stamp.
8. Cut a piece of scrap card stock 1⅝ × 2⅝ inches (4.1 × 6.7 cm). Stamp the party stamp in the center, then outline its edge with a brush marker. Use foam dots to attach it to the front of the card below the cake.
9. Run a brush marker against a ruler's edge to create a narrow border around the entire card.

PARTY HAT

1. Cut a template from a piece of blank newsprint, then use it to cut the gift wrap.
2. Ink any of the stamps on the materials list with brush markers and stamp them on the gift wrap. Outline its bottom edge with a brush marker.
3. Cover both sides of the stamped gift wrap with contract paper. Trim off any excess.
4. Shape the paper into a cone, then secure it with staples. Staple the ends of a piece of elastic cord to each side of the hat.

ROMANTIC VALENTINE'S DAY COLLAGE

Collages are two-dimensional compositions made of paper, fabric, and other materials that have been glued to a surface. Valentine's Day greetings were among the many popular forms of collage that preceded its emergence as a fine art medium in the early 20th century. The Victorian-style collage shown below combines delicately colored and embossed rubber stamp images with paper lace, a handmade envelope, and a brass trinket. Surprise your loved one by sending him or her a love note in the miniature envelope.

MATERIALS
Stamps
Pansy blossom (308C)
Rose frame (619E)
Small bow (A739D)
Inks and Embossing Powders
Chocolate brown pigment ink stamp pad
Purple pigment ink stamp pad
Clear embossing powder
Gold embossing powder
Brush Markers
Light green
Dusty pink
Bright yellow
Papers
Two pale rose postcards
One cream parchment postcard
Embellishments
Brass trinket
Oval paper doily
Miscellaneous
Scissors
Embossing heat tool
Glue stick
Ruler
Bone folder
Glue gun
Gold metallic pen

1. Stamp pansies on three corners of one of the pale rose postcards, two in chocolate brown and one in purple. Sprinkle them with clear embossing powder, tap off the excess, then melt with an embossing heat tool.

2. Use the brush markers to color the pansies. Use bright yellow for the centers of the flowers, dusty pink for the rest of the petals, and light green for the leaves, blending colors as you work. Apply more ink where deeper shades are desired.

3. On the cream parchment postcard, stamp two pansies in purple pigment ink and one rose frame and one bow in brown pigment ink. Emboss the pansies and the rose frame with clear embossing powder and the bow with gold embossing powder. Color the images with brush markers, then cut them out and set them aside. (See Photo 1.)

4. Lay the doily over the pale rose postcard so that it slightly overlaps all three pansies. Trim the doily to the dimensions of the postcard, then glue it to the postcard with the glue stick. (See Photo 2.)

5. Cut a 4¹/₂-inch (11.4-cm) square from the other pale rose postcard. Make an envelope by folding the corners into the center of the card so that the edges of the flaps overlap slightly. Use the pointed edge of the bone folder to make sharp creases. Glue the bottom three flaps together at the edges with the glue stick, then glue the small bow to the top flap of the envelope. (See Photo 3.)

6. Position the envelope at an angle over the doily. Use the glue gun to glue two pansies to the doily so that they're partially covered by the envelope. Glue the envelope to the doily, the rose frame in the top right-hand corner of the card, and the brass trinket in lower right-hand corner.

7. Insert a miniature love note into the envelope. Write your true love's name in the rose frame with a gold metallic pen.

1

2

3

CALLA LILY NOTECARD

This elegant notecard, which can be used as an invitation to a bridal shower or an intimate wedding, simulates cast paper by combining blind embossing, rubber stamping, and puff paint. In contrast to thermal embossing, which heats slow-drying ink and embossing powder to obtain a raised image, blind embossing produces a raised image on paper by tracing its outline with a sharp instrument. To achieve a smooth, matte finish reminiscent of cast paper, puff paint must be allowed to dry for 24 hours prior to heating. While puff-painted images are quite attractive in white, they can also be tinged with watercolor to add a soft hint of color.

MATERIALS

Stamps
Classic calla lily (Z431E)

Inks
Black pigment ink stamp
pad
Pale yellow brush marker

Papers
For one notecard
One white, uncoated
prefolded notecard
One piece of cardboard,
cut to the dimensions of
the closed notecard

Miscellaneous
Scrap paper
Scissors
Stamp cleaner
Paper towels
Metal ruler
Pencil
Cutting mat
Craft knife
Light table *or* light-filled
window
Artist's tape
Tracing paper
Bone folder
White puff paint
Embossing heat tool

1. Ink the stamp with black pigment ink and stamp it on the scrap paper. Cut the print out. Clean the stamp with stamp cleaner and paper towels.

2. To create the blind embossing template, position the scrap-paper print on the cardboard. Use the ruler and a pencil to draw a vertically oriented rectangle around it, leaving an equal margin of space around the top and sides to the edge of the cardboard. Cut the rectangle out by placing the cardboard on a cutting mat, aligning the edge of the ruler with each of the rectangle's sides, and running the tip of the craft knife against it.

3. Affix the cardboard template to the light table with artist's tape. (See Photo 1.) If you don't have access to a light table, tape the template to a window that's illuminated by daylight.

4. Open the notecard and place its cover face down on the template. To protect the card's finish, cover it with a piece of tracing paper. Using the blunt end of the bone folder, rub the notecard from the center outward to gently push it down into the template. Use the pointed edge of the bone folder to crease the notecard at the edges of the template. When you've made a complete impression of the template, remove the notecard. (See Photo 2.)

5. Ink the stamp with the brush marker. Blot it once on a piece of scrap paper, then remoisten the inks by breathing on the die. Stamp the image so that it's centered within the embossed rectangle on the front of the card. Let dry. (See Photo 3.)

6. Apply puff paint to the entire stamped image, spreading it with the tip of the applicator so that it looks like smooth cake icing and leaving the small open areas of the print exposed. Let dry for 24 hours, then use the embossing heat tool to puff the paint. (See Photo 4.)

7. Repeat steps 4 through 6 to make additional notecards.

1

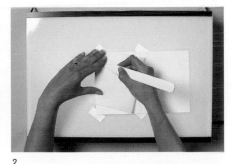

2

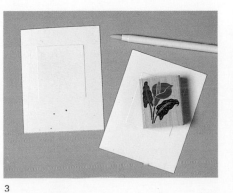

3

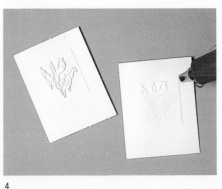

4

131

HALLOWEEN POP-UP CARD

The mischief of Halloween initiates the festivities of the autumn and winter, and this playful pop-up card can provide an easy way to mark the start of the season. Simple folding techniques, several kinds of glue, and embellishments of raffia and glitter are used to create depth and dimension. The materials list and instructions are for one card, but an assembly-line approach for a large mailing—folding, embossing, stamping, cutting, and gluing—can accelerate the process.

MATERIALS
Stamps
Spider web (Z140C)
Happy Halloween (Z503E)
Wolf (A841E)
Plump pumpkin (Z282C)
Toothy grin (Z318A)
Bare tree (Z283F)
Inks and Embossing Powders
Embossing ink stamp pad
Silver embossing powder
Black pigment ink stamp pad
Clear embossing powder
Chocolate brown pigment ink stamp pad
Brush Markers
Gray
Pale orange
Red
Orange
Green
Bright yellow
Papers
To make one pop-up card
Two black folded notecards
Two white, glossy coated postcards
A sheet of sticker paper
Embellishments
Opalescent glitter
Raffia
Silver stars
Miscellaneous
Ruler
Bone folder
Post-it notes
Embossing heat tool
Scissors
Wedge-shaped foam sponge
Glue pen
Glue stick
Glue gun
Foam dots

1. Use the ruler and the bone folder to score a parallel crease 1 inch (2.5 cm) from the mountain fold of one of the black notecards. Repeat on the other side of the fold. (See Photo 1.)

2. Mask the area between one of the score lines and the fold with Post-its. Use clear embossing ink and silver embossing powder to stamp and emboss a spider web border on that side of the notecard. Remove the masks and repeat on the other side.

3. Use clear embossing ink and silver embossing powder to stamp and emboss the Happy Halloween stamp in the center of one side of the notecard.

4. Use black pigment ink and clear embossing powder to stamp and emboss the wolf on a white postcard, then color it with gray and pale orange brush markers.

5. Ink the pumpkin stamp with the red and orange markers, then ink the stem with the green marker. Stamp it on the white postcard. Repeat to stamp a second single pumpkin.

6. To create a pair of pumpkins, ink the stamp as directed in step 5, then stamp it on the white postcard. Prepare a mask of the pumpkin, then use it to cover the print. Re-ink and stamp the pumpkin at an angle next to the first. Repeat to stamp another pair.

7. Use black pigment ink and clear embossing powder to stamp and emboss a grin on each of the single pumpkins and on the foreground pumpkin in each pair.

8. Ink the sponge with the yellow marker, apply it to the other white postcard in a 2-inch (5-cm) square area, then cut a circle from it to make a moon. Use the glue pen to accent the moon and the pumpkins's grins with opalescent glitter.

9. Use brown pigment ink and clear embossing powder to stamp and emboss the tree on sticker paper. Use scissors to cut out the tree and all the images stamped on white postcard.

10. Apply the glue stick to the back of the scored notecard, avoiding the area between the two score lines. (See Photo 2.) Glue the scored notecard to the inside of the second notecard, aligning the cards at the edges.

11. Cut the raffia into small, irregular pieces. Use the glue gun to affix them in clusters to the backs of the pumpkins.

12. Remove the backing from the tree and stick it on the right-hand side of the notecard opposite the greeting. Use a foam dot to adhere the moon to the top left-hand side. Stack two foam dots, apply them to the back of the wolf, then adhere the wolf to the card so that it's silhouetted against the moon. Use the glue gun to affix a pair of pumpkins to the right of the wolf. Apply a foam dot to the back of one of the single pumpkins, then position it to the right of the pair. Use the glue gun to affix the remaining pumpkins on the left-hand side of the lower part of the pop-up ledge. Adhere the glitter stars randomly to the card with the glue pen.

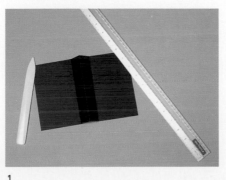

1

2

CHRISTMAS ORNAMENT CARD

For many people, Christmas is the only time of the year for which written greetings are conveyed. This triple die-cut greeting card, which features two rubber stamp images, brush markers, gold glitter embossing powder, and a gold ribbon, is surprisingly simple to make, and will undoubtedly impress your family and friends. Use a single card to grace a mantelpiece or prominent windowsill with holiday cheer.

MATERIALS
Stamps
Starflake ornament
(A1047H)
Posh pine (Z151C)
Inks
Embossing ink stamp
pad
Brush Markers
Green
Light green
Violet
Bright red
Bright yellow
Embossing Powders
Gold glitter embossing
powder
Papers
For one card
One 6- × 13¹/₂-inch
(15.2- × 34.3-cm) piece
of white, glossy coated
cardstock
Embellishments
Narrow gold ribbon
Miscellaneous
Pencil
Ruler
Bone folder
Stamp positioning tool
Tracing paper
Stamp cleaner
Paper towels
Craft knife
Cutting mat
Embossing heat tool
Gold ribbon
Glue gun

1. Use a pencil to lightly mark the card into three equal sections, each measuring 4¹/₂ inches (11.43 cm) wide. Align the ruler with one of the lines, then score it with the pointed edge of the bone folder. Repeat with the other two pencil lines.

2. Using any of the brush markers, the stamp positioning tool, and a piece of tracing paper, create a tracing-paper template for the ornament stamp. Clean the stamp with stamp cleaner and paper towels.

3. Center the tracing-paper template on the left-hand section of the card. Ink the ornament stamp with embossing ink. Align the corner of the stamp positioning tool with the corner of the template, remove the template, and stamp the ornament by aligning its block with the corner of the positioning tool. Sprinkle the image with gold glitter embossing powder, tap off the excess, and melt with the embossing heat tool. (See photo below.) Repeat this step for the other two sections of the card.

4. Color the ornaments with the brush markers. The predominant color for the first ornament should be violet, the second red, and the third green.

5. Ink the pine stamp with the light green brush marker and stamp it randomly to create a wide border, re-inking after making each print. Ink the stamp with the medium green marker and repeat this step, overlapping some of the lighter green prints.

6. Use the ruler and the bone folder to score a line above and below the center of each ornament. Use the craft knife to die-cut the right side of each.

7. Crease the score lines to make the first, third, and fifth scores mountain folds, and the second and fourth scores valley folds.

8. Attach the gold ribbon to the card with the glue gun.

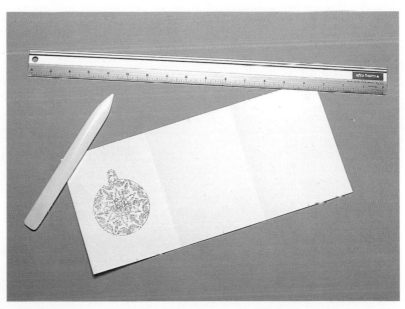

GINGERBREAD APRON

Since the holidays always mean time spent preparing special treats, you can make your kitchen duty more festive by dressing in the spirit of the season. Stamp and paint a plain cotton apron with a cheerful regiment of gingerbread men brandishing candy canes and decked with sprigs of holly. Puff-painted "icing" and gold glitter bow ties provide lighthearted finishing touches.

MATERIALS

Project
Buff-colored canvas apron

Stamps
Big gingerbread man (A1053F)
Christmas holly (Z153C)

Inks
Black dye-based ink stamp pad
Black fabric ink stamp pad
Bright red fabric ink re-inker
Emerald green fabric ink re-inker

Textile Markers
Red

Paints
Ginger brown fabric paint
Gold dimensional fabric paint
White puff paint

Miscellaneous
Blank newsprint
Scrap paper
Stamp positioning tool
Tracing paper
Stamp cleaner
Paper towels
Two wedge-shaped foam sponges (one for each re-inker bottle)
Small paint brush

VARIATIONS
Save your scrap-paper prints to design gingerbroad and holly placemats, napkins, or gift wrap.

1. Cover your work surface with several pieces of blank newsprint.
2. Using black dye-based ink, stamp fifteen gingerbread men and fifty-four holly sprigs on scrap paper. Cut the prints out and use them to lay out the design shown on the opposite page. (See also Photo 1.)
3. Use black dye-based ink and the stamp positioning tool to make a template for each stamp. Clean the stamps with stamp cleaner and paper towels. Except for the first and second rows of gingerbread men, remove all of the scrap-paper prints from the apron.
4. Ink the gingerbread man stamp with black fabric ink. Cover one of the scrap-paper prints with the tracing-paper template, then align the corner of the stamp positioning tool with the corner of the template. Remove both the print and the template, then stamp the gingerbread man by aligning the corner of its block with the corner of the positioning tool. (See Photo 2.)
5. Repeat step 4 for the remaining gingerbread men in the top and center rows. Return the scrap-paper prints for the bottom row of gingerbread men to the apron, then repeat until all have been stamped.
6. Return the holly prints to the apron. Ink a sponge with red fabric ink, then dab it on the berries portion of the holly stamp's die. Ink the other sponge with green fabric ink and dab it on the leaves. Use the positioning tool and the holly template to stamp the remaining holly sprigs as directed in step 4, re-inking the stamp after making each print. (See Photo 3.) Let dry overnight.
7. Paint the gingerbread men with brown fabric paint, leaving the hair, mouths, bow ties, buttons, icing stripes, and candy canes blank. (See Photo 4.) Let dry.
8. Use the red textile marker to color the mouths, buttons, and candy cane stripes. Follow the manufacturer's instructions to heat-set the inks.
9. Apply white puff paint sparingly to the hair and icing stripes. Let dry for 24 hours, then use the embossing heat tool to puff the paint.
10. Apply gold dimensional paint to the bow ties.

1

2

3

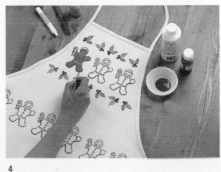

4

QUILTED HOLIDAY STOCKINGS

A color scheme of red, green, and gold inevitably evokes the winter holidays. The stockings shown below are stamped with flowers, but their colors are undeniably those of the Christmas season. To make a quick gift or enduring keepsake, these quilted stockings can be decorated with just about any large stamp design, colored with red and green textile markers, and embellished with quilting stitches and shimmering gold dimensional fabric paint.

MATERIALS
Pattern
Page 155

MATERIALS
Pattern
Page 155
Stamps
For the tulip stocking
Tulip designs (773H)
Wandering vine large roller (R303)
Inks
Black dye-based ink stamp pad
Black fabric ink stamp pad
Textile Markers
Red
Dark teal
Light violet
Yellow
Fabric Paints
Gold glitter dimensional fabric paint
Fabrics
To make two stockings
1½ yards (54- × 45-inch [137.2 × 114.3-cm] piece) of muslin
1½ yards (54- × 45-inch [137.2 × 114.3-cm] piece) of thin, lightweight batting
Stitching Supplies
Cream-colored thread
Red or green bias tape
Miscellaneous
Scissors
Scrap paper
Stamp positioning tool
Tracing paper
Blank newsprint
Stamp cleaner
Paper towels

VARIATIONS
To create the rose stocking (see opposite), randomly stamp the rose design (771H) with black fabric ink on the right side of one of the stocking shapes. Allow the prints to dry before coloring with textile markers. Machine-quilt the outlines of the roses, assemble the stocking, then embellish with swirls of dimensional fabric paint.

TULIP STOCKING

1. Enlarge the pattern to full size.
2. Fold the fabric in half wrong sides together, then position the pattern. Choose the stocking's orientation, then cut through both layers to cut a pair of stocking shapes (for one side of the stocking); reposition the pattern and repeat to cut a second pair. Cut two stocking shapes from the batting.
3. Using black dye-based ink, stamp five tulips on scrap paper and cut them out. Use black dye-based ink and the stamp positioning tool to make a tracing-paper template. Clean the stamp with stamp cleaner and paper towels.
4. Place one of the stocking shapes on a sheet of blank newsprint. Use the prints to lay out the design shown on the opposite page. Ink the tulip stamp with black fabric ink. Cover one of the prints with the template, then align the corner of the positioning tool with the corner of the template. Remove both the print and the template, then stamp a tulip by aligning the corner of its block with the corner of the positioning tool. Repeat for the four remaining tulips.
5. Ink the roller stamp with black fabric ink. Use the long edge of the positioning tool to guide the path of the print, which should run off the edges of the stocking. Hold down the tool with one hand to keep it in place. (See photo below.) Repeat for the two remaining borders.
6. Allow the ink to dry, then color the prints with the textile markers. Let dry. If necessary, heat-set the inks as indicated in the manufacturer's instructions.
7. Layer the stamped stocking shape, one piece of batting, and a plain stocking shape. Pin the sandwich at several points to keep the layers from slipping. Machine-quilt a line of stitches on either side of the roller prints, removing the pins as you work. On the stamped side of the sandwich, machine-baste the raw edges of the bias tape and the stocking together.
8. Layer another piece of batting between two stocking shapes. Pin the sandwich, then machine-baste it at the seam line. Position the two sandwiches right sides together. Pin, then sew, all the layers together at the seam lines, leaving the top of the stocking open. Turn the stocking inside out.
9. Pin the bias tape to the stamped layer of the stocking, raw edges together. Use a scrap piece of muslin as facing, then sew it to sandwich the bias tape between the stocking and the facing. Turn the facing inward and slipstitch it to the inside of stocking. Make a loop out of a piece of bias tape and slipstitch it to the inside of the stocking.
10. Embellish the printed stocking with dimensional paint. Let dry.

DIMENSIONAL PARTRIDGE PICTURE

Dimensional rubber stamping techniques are often used to make fun, lighthearted images (see page 52 for a few examples). In this project, these techniques are used to create a graceful decorative holiday accent that features traditional iconography while avoiding the conventional red-and-green color scheme. Our completed partridge is matted within a 5- × 7-inch (12.7- × 17.8-cm) window of dark green silk shantung and framed in an 8- × 10-inch (20.3- × 25.4-cm) gold frame.

MATERIALS
Stamps
Partridge (A1039G)
Inks
Black pigment ink stamp pad
Papers
Cream-colored parchment card stock
Colored Pencils
For the partridge
Terracotta
Brown
Gray
For the leaves
Medium green
Olive green
For the pear
Yellow
Orange
Miscellaneous
Pencil
Craft knife
Cutting mat
Teaspoon
Glue gun *or* silicone sealer

1. Trim the paper to the dimensions of the mat window, adding approximately 1 inch (2.5 cm) to the length and width.
2. Place the paper under the mat. Use a pencil to lightly outline its window.
3. Ink the stamp with black pigment ink and stamp it in the center of the outline. Let dry thoroughly before coloring the print with colored pencils. If needed, use the stamp's index as a guide. (See Photo 1.)
4. Re-inking the stamp after making each print, use the black pigment ink to stamp six more partridges on another piece of parchment paper. Let dry. On one of the images, color the partridge's wing, all five leaves, and the foreground pear. (See Photo 2.) In the remaining five images, color twelve individual leaves. (If you would like to layer other areas, color them as well.)
5. Positioning each image on the cutting mat, use the craft knife to carefully cut out the partridge's wing, the pear, and the leaves, trimming just outside the outlines of each image. (See Photo 3.)
6. Place the pear cutout right side down in the palm of your hand and rub it with the bowl of a spoon to gently curve the paper. (See Photo 4.) Repeat with the remaining cutouts.
7. Apply a small amount of glue or silicone sealer to the back of each of the cutouts. (See Photo 5.) Carefully place the partridge's wing, the pear, and the five leaves over their counterparts in the intact partridge image.
8. Cluster three leaves together and glue the cluster in one of the corners of the image area. Repeat for the three remaining corners. (See Photo 6.)
9. Erase the window's outline. Mat and frame the image as desired.

1

2

3

4

5

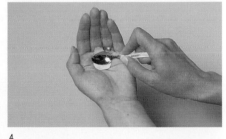

6

DÉCOUPAGE ANGEL TRAY

The art of découpage (from the French *decouper,* "to cut out") emerged in Europe in the late 17th century, inspired by intricately ornamented and heavily lacquered furniture from China and Japan. Paper motifs are carefully cut out, glued to a surface in a pleasing arrangement, then coated with several layers of varnish. While a wide range of discarded printed materials has served as the traditional source for découpage images, rubber stamps can be used to create images for a specific project, as was done for the tray shown below. Découpage takes some time and patience, but the results are well worth the effort. A beautiful gold-trimmed tray can provide an elegant finishing touch for any holiday table, or make a thoughtful gift.

MATERIALS

Project
Unfinished wood tray with handles

Stamps
Grand angel (A1075G)
Sweet angel (A1071D)
Victorian star (A1072C)

Inks and Embossing Powders
Chocolate brown pigment ink
Clear embossing powder
Embossing ink stamp pad
Gold embossing powder

Paints
For the tray
Burgundy acrylic paint
Gold metallic acrylic paint
For the stamps
Watercolor paints in various colors (see instructions)

Brushes
Two medium-sized brushes (one to apply the burgundy paint, the other to apply the decoupage glue)
Two small brushes (one to apply the gold metallic paint, the other to brush off excess embossing powder)

Papers
Cream-colored paper

Miscellaneous
Sandpaper
Tack cloth
Artist's tape
Cuticle or small scissors
Pencil
Embossing heat tool
Découpage glue
Découpage varnish

PREPARING THE TRAY

1. Sand the tray until smooth, then wipe it lightly with the tack cloth.
2. Basecoat the tray with burgundy paint. Let dry thoroughly. Paint the top edge of the tray and the insides of the handles with gold metallic paint.
3. Use artist's tape to create a ¼-inch (0.64-cm) rectangular border in the center of the tray. (The inner dimensions of the rectangle should measure 5½ × 8½ inches [13.8 × 21.6 cm].) Paint the border with the gold paint, let dry, then carefully remove the tape. (See Photo 1.)

STAMPING, EMBOSSING, AND PAINTING

4. Using chocolate brown pigment ink, stamp three large and ten small angels on cream-colored paper. Emboss them with clear embossing powder.
5. Paint the embossed angels with watercolors, using the photo opposite as a guide. Pink, green, yellow, and gold were used here. (See Photo 2.)
6. Cut out each angel with cuticle scissors, trimming the edges carefully. Arrange the angel cutouts on the tray as shown opposite. Use a pencil to lightly mark the center of the space between the angels, then set them aside.
7. Ink the star stamp with embossing ink, position the center of the star over a pencil mark, and stamp. Sprinkle the star with gold embossing powder, then tap off the excess. Use a clean small brush to remove any stray flecks of powder. Melt the powder with the embossing heat tool. Repeat this step for the remaining stars. (See Photo 3.)

DÉCOUPAGE AND FINISHING

8. Use the découpage glue to paste each angel in place. Let dry. (See Photo 4.)
9. Paint a thin layer of découpage varnish over the entire tray. Let dry thoroughly.
10. Apply several layers of varnish to the surface of the tray, allowing each layer to dry before adding the next, until the images are embedded in the varnish and the surface of the tray is smooth and even.

1

2

3

4

PATTERNS AND DIAGRAMS

The pages that follow contain the patterns and diagrams necessary to complete eight of the projects in this book.

WORKING WITH PATTERNS

Since the dimensions of this book are too small to accommodate the patterns for most of the projects at full size, it will be necessary for you to enlarge them. The first step is to copy the pattern you want to use. There are several ways to do this, two of which are discussed below.

1. COPYING AND RESIZING WITH A PHOTOCOPIER

A photocopier with an enlargement feature is the easiest way to work with a pattern. With a photocopier, you can simultaneously copy the pattern *and* enlarge it to the size at which it is used for the project. Simply enter the percentage for enlargement that accompanies each pattern into the photocopier, then copy it from the book.

If you would prefer to use the pattern at another size than what was used in the book, either larger or smaller, use a calculator to compute the percentage for reduction or enlargement by dividing the intended pattern size by its current size.

- *Example 1: Enlarging.* If the pattern is 6 inches (15.2 cm) wide and needs to be $9^1/_2$ inches (24.1 cm) wide, you must enlarge it 1.58 times its current size ($9.5 \div 6 = 1.58$; $24.1 \div 15.2 = 1.58$), or photocopy it at 158 percent.
- *Example 2: Reducing.* If the pattern is 6 inches (15.2 cm) wide and needs to be $4^1/_2$ inches (11.4 cm) wide, you must reduce it 0.75 times its current size ($4.5 \div 6 = 0.75$; $11.4 \div 15.2 = 0.75$), or photocopy it at 75 percent.

If you don't have access to a photocopier, you'll have to trace and resize the pattern by hand as outlined below.

2. TRACING AND RESIZING WITH A PROPORTIONAL GRID

Copy the pattern by using a pencil to trace its outline onto a piece of tracing paper, then enlarge the copy by creating a proportional grid.

1. Draw a rectangle around the pattern, rounding its dimensions to the nearest unit of measurement (for example, use $^1/_8$, $^1/_4$, or $^1/_2$ inch for U.S. measurements; half or whole centimeters for metric measurements). Make sure that its corners are right angles.
2. Use a ruler to mark each unit along the length and width of the rectangle. Connect the marks to form a grid.
3. Sketch a second rectangle that corresponds roughly to the size you want the pattern to be. Draw the bottom and left line of the rectangle more firmly, extending them slightly beyond the outline.
4. So that the pattern will be enlarged or reduced in proportion to the traced copy, the rectangles that surround them must also have the same proportions, with corners that align on the diagonal. Place the smaller rectangle over the rough sketch, aligning them at their lower left-hand corners. Draw a diagonal line from the lower left-hand corner of the smaller rectangle through its upper right-hand corner, extending the line through the perimeter of the rough sketch.

5. Mark the point on the diagonal at which it intersects the rough sketch. To create the second rectangle, use a ruler to extend a line from the point to the left side of the rough sketch, then from the point to the bottom.
6. To make the grid, divide the second rectangle into the same number of squares as there are on the first one.
7. Draw the pattern on the new grid by copying the contents of each square from the original pattern.

To reduce a pattern, simply draw the image within a smaller grid.

TRANSFERRING A PATTERN TO A SURFACE

There are some projects for which you'll need to transfer a pattern directly to a surface. (The three box projects in this book require this step.) Begin by copying the correctly sized pattern onto tracing paper, then use one of the following transfer methods:

- *Retrace patterns lines with chalk, or rub the back of a pattern with chalk or pencil.* With the traced pattern face down, carefully retrace its lines using a chalk pencil (*not* a pastel pencil) or rub the entire pattern with a stick of chalk or a No. 2 pencil. Shake off any excess chalk or graphite dust, then lay the pattern, chalk or graphite side down, on the project. Using as little pressure as possible so you won't scratch or cut into your project's surface, retrace the pattern lines with the pointed end of a bone folder, a stylus, or a depleted ballpoint pen.
- *Use transfer paper.* Artist's transfer paper, which is sold under such brand names as Saral and Chacopaper, is made specifically for this purpose. One side of each sheet is treated with a water-soluble, erasable graphite-based material. Simply layer the transfer paper, treated side down, between the pattern and the project, and trace over the pattern lines. Although transfer paper is handled similarly to carbon paper, note that carbon paper should never be used to transfer a pattern to a surface.

WORKING WITH DIAGRAMS

A diagram is a small-scale graphic representation of the arrangement and relationships of a project's elements. In contrast to patterns, diagrams do not need to be resized or transferred to the surface of a project. Two of the stitching projects in this book are supported with diagrams that indicate the dimensions of each element.

JAPANESE PETAL BOX PATTERN

Project instructions are on pages 92–93.
Enlarge 125%.

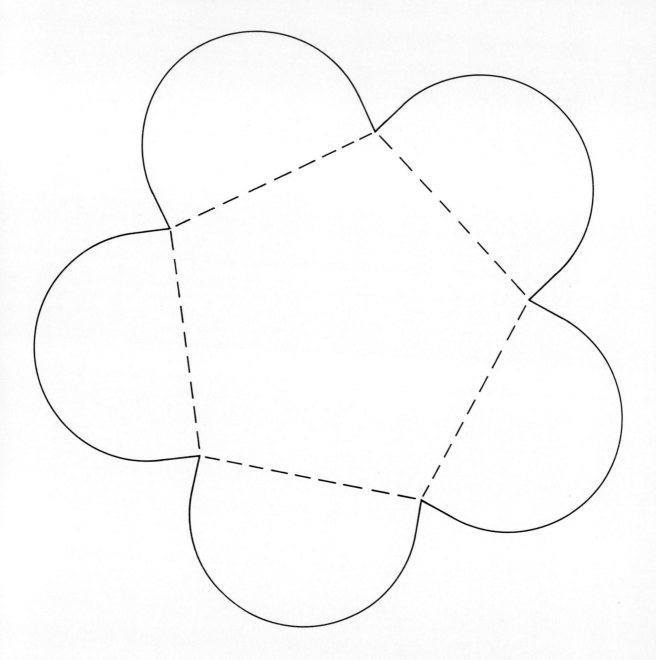

JAPANESE PYRAMID BOX PATTERN
Project instructions are on pages 92–93.
Enlarge 125%.

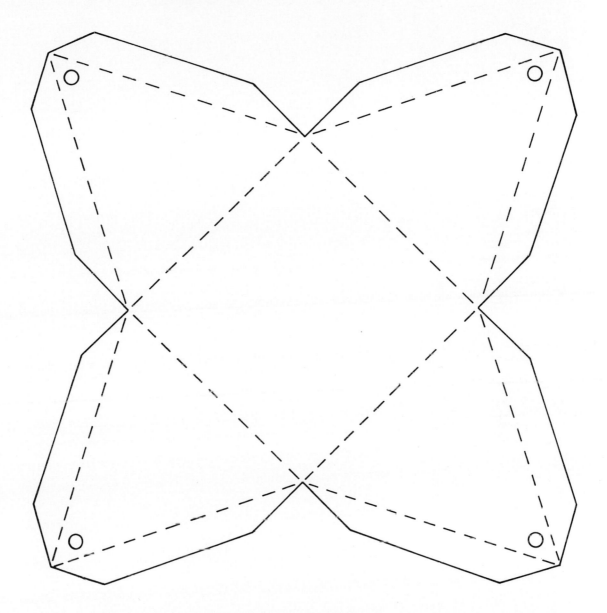

FERN STATIONERY GIFT BOX PATTERN

Project instructions are on pages 94–95.
Enlarge 200%.

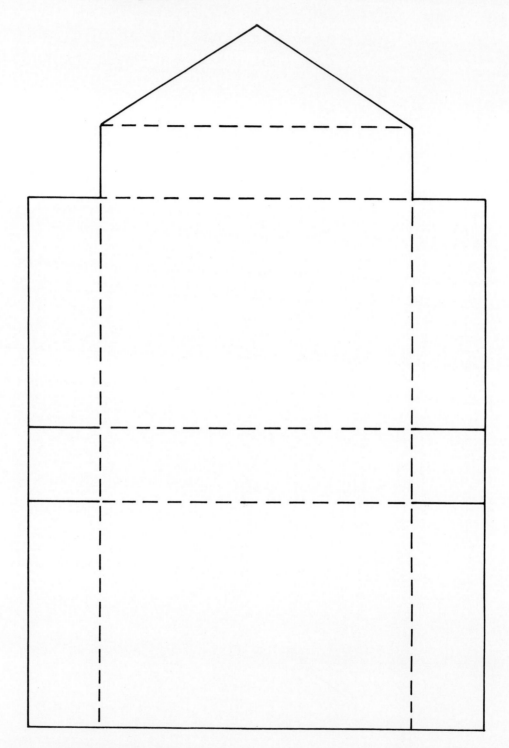

GARDEN WALL HANGING QUILTING DIAGRAM

Project instructions are on pages 112–113.

All measurements are in inches. The height of each quilted area is given first, then the width. The finished quilt measures 13½ inches (34.3 cm) square.

1. 1½ × 1½
2. 3¼ × 4¾
3. 6¼ × 1¼
4. 5¼ × 4
5. 3 × 4¾
6. 2½ × 6
7. 3½ × 4
8. 1¼ × 4¾
9. 1¼ × 5¼

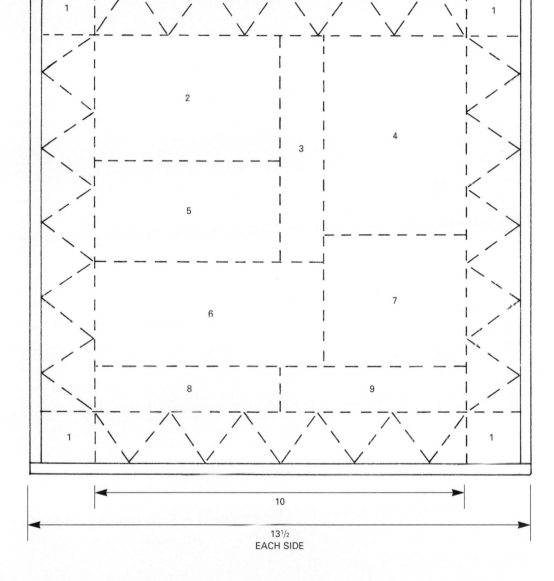

13½
EACH SIDE

PRIMITIVE ART WALL HANGING CUTTING AND PIECING DIAGRAM

Project instructions are on pages 116–117.

All measurements are in inches. The height of each piece is given first, then the width. Add ¼-inch (0.64-cm) seam allowance to all sides when measuring and cutting. The dimensions of the finished wall hanging are 16½ × 15½ inches (41.9 × 39.4 cm).

1. Beige
   4½ × 2
2. Rust
   4½ × 6½
3. Saffron
   4½ × 6½
4. Rust
   11½ × 2
5. Beige
   3 × 13
6. Saffron
   4½ × 5
7. Rust
   8½ × 3
8. Saffron
   4½ × 5
9. Beige
   4 × 5
10. Beige
    4 × 5

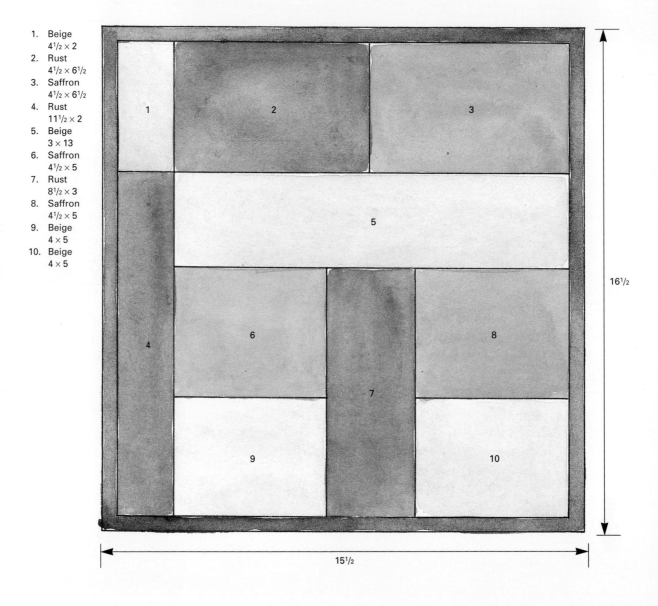

16½

15½

COUNTING SHEEP PILLOW FLANGE PATTERNS
Project instructions are on pages 118–120.
Use at same size. Patterns include ¼-inch (0.64-cm) seam allowance.

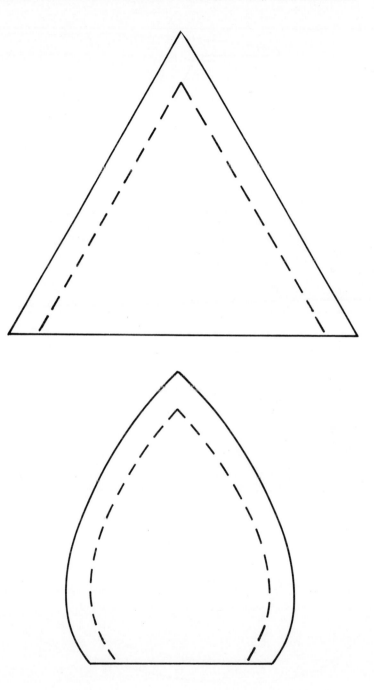

SOURCE DIRECTORY

Listed below are the manufacturers and wholesale suppliers for many of the materials used in this book. These companies generally sell their products exclusively to art supply, craft, and rubber stamping retailers, which are a consumer's most dependable sources for rubber stamping supplies. Your local retailer's knowledgeable personnel can advise you on your purchases, and if you need something that they don't have in stock they will usually order it for you. If you can't find a store in your area that carries a particular item or will accept a request for an order, or if you need special technical assistance, a manufacturer will gladly direct you to the retailer nearest you that carries their products, and will try to answer any other questions you might have. If you've exhausted all these avenues and still can't find what you're looking for, consult the publications listed below for mail-order sources.

Rubber Stamps
Rubber Stampede
P.O. Box 246
Berkeley, California 94701
(800) NEAT-FUN (632-8386)
Supplier for all the rubber stamp images used in this book. Corresponding item numbers are cited in the materials list for each project.

Creative Paperclay™
Creative Paperclay Company, Inc.
1800 South Robertson Boulevard
Suite 907
Los Angeles, California 90035
(310) 839-0466
Clay Button Wall Hanging, pages 121–23

Fabric Blanks
Bagworks, Inc.
3933 California Parkway
Fort Worth, Texas 96119
(817) 536-3892
Gingerbread Apron, pages 136–37

Make A Plate™ Kits
Makit Products, Inc.
4659 Mint Way
Dallas, Texas 75236
(214) 709-1606
Melamine Vegetable Plates, pages 86–87

Wood Products
Walnut Hollow
Route 2
Dodgeville, Wisconsin 53533
(608) 935-2341
Autumn Leaves Frame, pages 82–83
Butterfly Box, pages 84–85
Celestial Treasure Box, pages 105–7
Decoupage Angel Tray, pages 142–43

Textile Markers, Specialty Pens, and Other Art Supplies
EK Success Ltd.
611 Industrial Road
Carlstadt, NJ 07072
(800) 524-1349

Water-based Markers and Other Art Supplies
Marvy-Uchida
1027 East Burgrove Street
Carson, California 90746
(800) 541-5877

PUBLICATIONS
National Stampagraphic
19652 Sacramento Lane
Huntington Beach, California 92646-3223
(714) 968-4446
Published quarterly

Paper Crafters
6575 S.W. 86th Avenue
Portland, Oregon 97223
(503) 223-0167
Published quarterly

Rubber Stampers World Magazine
1390 Broadway
Suite B153
Placerville, California 95667
(916) 626-0874
Published bimonthly

Rubberstampmadness
P.O. Box 610
Corvallis, Oregon 97339
(503) 752-0075
Published bimonthly

INDEX

Absorbency, paper, 20
Achromatic colors, 42, 43
Acid-free papers, 20
Adhesives, 24–25
African wildlife gift wrap (project), 61–63
Analogous color schemes, 44
Angel tray, decoupage (project), 142–43
Animal skin print mats, embossed (project), 80–81
Apron, gingerbread (project), 136–37
Archival papers, 20
Art cards, watercolor (project), 74–75
Autumn leaves frame (project), 82–83

Backgrounds, 48, 56–57
Backprint, 14
Beet and carrot melamine plate (project), 87
Birthday party accessories (project), 126–27
Blank newsprint, 24, 25
Blending, color, 47
Block, 13
Bone folder, 25
Border-pattern T-shirt (project), 100–1
Borders, 39, 40, 58–59
Bordered stationery, rose (project), 71
Box(es) (projects)
    butterfly, 84–85
    celestial treasure, 105–7
    gift. See Gift box(es)
    recipe, 102–4
Brayer, 27, 29
Brayered backgrounds, 57
Broad-surface stamps, 12, 33
Brushes, paint, 25
Brush markers, 26, 27, 33, 47
Butterfly box (project), 84–85
Buttons, clay, 121–23 (project)

Calla lily notecard (project), 130–31
Calligraphy pens, 27, 28
Card(s) (projects). See also Notecard(s)
    Christmas ornament, 134–35
    Halloween pop-up, 132–33
    recipe, 104
    rose garland, 73
    stained glass grape, 64–65
    watercolor art, 74–75
Caring for stamps, 14
Celestial treasure box and gift tag (project), 105–7
Chalks, 27

Christmas ornament card (project), 134–35
Chroma, 42
Circles, designing with, 39
Circular patterns, 40
Clay button wall hanging (project), 121–23
Clear-mount stamps, 14
Clip file, 38
Coated papers, 20
Collage, Valentine's Day (project), 128–29
Color
    adding of, 46
    blending of, 47
    fundamentals of, 42–45
    and perception, 44
    working with, 46–47
Color accessories, 26–28
Color chord, 44
Colored pencils, 26, 27, 46
Color harmony, 44
Coloring, 46
Color schemes, 44–45
Color wheel, 42–43
Combining images, 50
    to suggest movement, 55
Complementary colors, 44, 45
Complementary color schemes, 44
Composition
    landscape or scene, 41
    layout, 38
Contrasts, color, 44
Cool colors, 42, 43, 45
Copyright law, 9
Corrections, 34
Counting sheep pillow (project), 118–20
Craft knife, 25
Craft punches, 25, 26
Creative Paperclay™, 23, 121–23 (project)
Cushion, 13
Cutting, paper, 37
Cutting mat, 24, 25
Cutting tools, 24

Decor, home, 79–89
Decorative-edge scissors, 59
Decorative terracotta tiles, 22, 23, 88–89 (project)
Découpage angel tray (project), 142–43
Density, paper, 20
Depth, 45, 51–52
Design strategies, 38–41
Diagrams, 146, 147

Die, 13
Dimension, 28–29, 51, 52
Dimensional fabric paint, 29
Dimensional partridge picture (project),
        140–41
Dots, foam, 29
Dragging, 53
Dye-based ink rainbow pads, 18
Dye-based inks, 16–17

Earrings, tulip quilt block (project), 77
Edges, 58, 59
Embossed animal skin print mats (project),
        80–81
Embossing, 36, 58
Embossing heat tool, 25, 36
Embossing inks, 17, 36
Embossing powders, 27, 28, 36, 47
Envelope, rose-trimmed (project), 71
Erasers, 25
Extent, contrasts of, 44

Fabric inks, 17
Fabric paint, dimensional, 29
Fabrics, 21–22
Fading out, 53, 54
Fair use of stamp images, 9
Felt stamp pads, 32
Fern frame and gift wrap (project), 96–97
Fern stationery and gift box (project),
        94–95
Fine-point markers, 27
Foam dots and tape, 29
Foam-handled stamps, 13–14
Foam sponges, 25, 27, 46, 47
Foam stamp pads, 32
Folding, paper, 37
Frame (projects)
    autumn leaves, 82–83
    fern, 96–97

Garden wall hanging (project), 112–13
Ghosting, 57
Gift box(es) (projects)
    fern, 94, 95
    Japanese paper, 92–93
Gift ideas, 91–107
Gift set, recipe box (project), 102–4
Gift tag(s) (projects)
    celestial, 105, 106
    giraffe, 63
    recipe, 104
Gift wrap (projects)
    African wildlife, 62–63
    fern, 96, 97
    hydrangea, 66–67

Gingerbread apron (project), 136–37
Giraffe wrapping paper and gift tag
        (project), 63
Glass, 22, 23
Glitter glue pens, 27, 28
Glitters, 27, 28, 29
Glues, 24–25
Gold metallic pens, 28
Grain, paper, 37
Grouping, 40

Half-drop repeat, 41
Halloween pop-up card (project), 132–33
Hand-drawn flourishes, 54
Hanging. See Wall hanging
Hole punches, 25, 26
Holidays, 125–45
Holiday stockings, quilted (project),
        138–39
Home decor, 79–89
Hot plate, 36
Hue, 42, 44
Hydrangea gift wrap (project), 66–67

Ideas, gathering of, 38
Inking, 32–33
Inks, 16–17
Intensity, color, 42, 44, 45
Invitation, New Year's Eve party (project),
        144–45
Iron, 36
Isolating part of image, 49, 58

Japanese journal (project), 98–99
Japanese paper gift boxes (project), 92–93
Jewelry, paper (project), 76–77
Journal
    for design ideas, 38
    Japanese, 98–99 (project)

Knives, 25

Labels, recipe (project), 104
Landscapes, 41, 45
Layout, 38
Leather, 22, 23
Leaves. See Autumn leaves frame
Linen and lace Victorian posy pillow
        (project), 110–11

Maintenance, stamp, 14
Make A Plate™, 86–87 (project)
Markers, 26, 27, 28, 47
    inking a stamp with, 33
Masks
    preparation of, 48

Masking, 48–50
    for borders, 58
    for motion, 54
Materials, 11–29
Mats, embossed animal skin print (*project*), 80–81
Melamine vegetable plates (*project*), 86–87
Miniature pieced quilt (*project*), 114–15
Mixed-pattern notecard (*project*), 68–69
Monochromatic color schemes, 44
Mortise masking, 49
Motion, 53–55
Mount, 13
Mountain fold, 37

Narrow borders and edges, 59
Newsprint, 24, 25
New Year's Eve party invitation (*project*), 144–45
Notecard(s) (*projects*). *See also* Card(s)
    calla lily, 130–31
    mixed-pattern, 68–69
    "Thinking of You," 72
Novelty borders and edges, 59
Novelty-edge scissors, 27, 28
Novelty shapes, 26

Observation, 38
One-color stamp pads, inking with, 32
Opaque inks, 16, 17
Organizing, 14–15
Orientation, 39, 40
Outline stamps, 12
Overprinting, 51

Paint brushes, 25
Paints, 27, 29
Palette, 44
Paper
    in masking, 50
    projects using, 61–77
    as stamping surface, 19–20
    working with, 37
Paper gift boxes, Japanese (*project*), 92–93
Paper jewelry (*project*), 76–77
Parameters, design, 39
Partridge picture, dimensional (*project*), 140–41
Party accessories, birthday (*project*), 126–27
Party invitation, New Year's Eve (*project*), 144–45
Patterns, 39–41, 57, 146–55. *See also* Diagrams
    enlarging and reducing, 146–47
    mixed, 68–69
    transferring, 147

Pattern stamp, for borders, 58
Pencils, 25, 26, 27, 46
Pens, 27, 28
Perception, color and, 44
Permanent inks, 16, 17
Pigment ink rainbow pads, 18
Pigment inks, 16, 17
Pillow (*projects*)
    counting sheep, 118–20
    Victorian posy, 110–11
Plaids, 57
Plastic, 23
Plates, melamine vegetable (*project*), 86–87
Pop-up card, Halloween (*project*), 132–33
Porcelain, 23
Positioning, 25, 26, 34–35, 58
Post-it™ notes, 25, 26
Posy pillow, Victorian (*project*), 110–11
Pots, terracotta, 22, 23
Primary colors, 42, 43
Primitive art wall hanging (*project*), 116–17
Puff paint, 27, 29
Punches, 25, 26

Quilting (*projects*)
    garden wall hanging, 112–13
    holiday stockings, 138–39
    miniature pieced, 114–15

Rainbow stamp pads, 16, 18, 33
Recipe box gift set (*project*), 102–4
Rectangles, 39
Red rose stationery set (*project*), 70–73
Re-inkers, 16, 18
Relief, 28
Repeats, 40–41
Roller stamps, 14, 58
Romantic Valentine's Day collage (*project*), 128–29
Rose. *See* Red rose stationery set
Rotation, 39
Rubber brayer, 27, 29
Rubber stamps. *See* Stamp(s)
Rulers, 24, 25

Saturation, color, 42
Scallop-edge scissors, 59
Scenes, 41, 50
Scissors, 25, 27, 28, 59
Secondary colors, 42, 43
Shade, color, 42
Shadows, 51
Shared-mount stamps, 14
Sheep. *See* Counting sheep pillow
Shrink Plastic™, 23
Silver metallic pens, 28

Sizing, 20
Sketchbook, 38
Small stamp pads, 16, 18
Spacing, 38, 39
Special occasions, 125–45
Specialty pens, 28
Split-complementary color schemes, 44
Sponged backgrounds, 56
Sponges, 25, 27, 46, 47, 58, 59. *See also*
    Foam entries
Square repeat, 40, 41
Squares, designing with, 39
Stained glass grape card *(project)*, 64–65
Stamp(s)
    anatomy of, 12–13
    basics of, 12–15
    care and maintenance of, 14
    inking of, 32–33
    making of, 13
    positioning of, 34–35
    types of, 13–14
Stamped watercolor art cards *(project)*,
    74–75
Stamping
    for stitchers, 109–23
    surfaces for, 19–23
    techniques of, 31–59
Stamp pads, 16, 17–18, 47
    inking with, 32–33
Stamp positioning tool, 25, 26, 58
Stationery *(projects)*
    fern, 94–95
    red rose, 70–73
Stencils, 26
Stickers, 26
Stitchers, stamping for, 109–23
Stockings, quilted holiday *(project)*, 138–39
Storing, 14–15
Streaking, 53
Stylus, 25
Supplies, 11–29
Surfaces, stamping, 19–23

Tags. *See* Gift tag(s)
Tape, foam, 29
Tearing, paper, 37
Techniques, 31–59

Temperature, color, 42, 44, 45
Terracotta, 22, 23, 88–89 *(project)*
Tertiary colors, 42, 43
Tetradic color schemes, 44
Textile markers, 27, 28
Texture, tools for, 28–29
Textured backgrounds, 56
Texture stamp, for borders, 58
"Thinking of You" notecard *(project)*, 72
Tiles, terracotta, 22, 23, 88–89 *(project)*
Tint, 42
Tone, 42
Tools, 24–29
Tracing paper, 25, 26, 50
Translucent inks, 16, 17
Tray, découpage angel *(project)*, 142–43
Treasure box, celestial *(project)*, 105–7
Triadic color schemes, 44
Trinket embellishments, 27
T-shirt, border-pattern *(project)*, 100–1
Tube wringer, 27, 29
Tulip quilt block earrings *(project)*, 77

Uncoated papers, 20
Uninked stamp pads, 16, 18

Valentine's Day collage *(project)*, 128–29
Valley fold, 37
Value, color, 42, 44
Vegetable plates, melamine *(project)*,
    86–87
Victorian posy pillow *(project)*, 110–11
Vulcanizer, 13

Wall hanging *(projects)*
    clay button, 121–23
    primitive art, 116–17
    quilted garden, 112–13
Warm colors, 42, 43, 45
Washable inks, 16
Watercolor art cards *(project)*, 74–75
Watercolor pencils, 27
Watercolors, 26–27, 46
Wearables, 39 *(project)*
White correction pens, 28
Wood, 20–21, 22
Wrapping paper. *See* Gift wrap